ECONOMICS IN THE FUTURE

ECONOMICS IN THE FUTURE

Edited by

Kurt Dopfer

Professor of Economics
International
Christian University
Tokyo, Japan

M

First published 1976 by
THE MACMILLAN PRESS LTD
London and Basingstoke
Associated companies in New York Dublin
Melbourne Johannesburg and Madras

SBN 333 19502 7 (hard cover)
333 19503 5 (paper cover)

Set at the Universities Press, Belfast, Northern Ireland
and printed at The Pitman Press, Bath

Contents

Contents

Notes on Contributors

KURT DOPFER has been Visiting Professor at the International Christian University, Tokyo, 1972–5, on leave from St Gall School of Economics and Social Science, St Gallen (Switzerland). His publications include *Theory of Convergence, Theory of Long Term Changes of Economic Systems* and *Relationship between Population and Development.* He is currently conducting research on socio-economic development in Asia with the support of the Asia Foundation and the Swiss National Fund for Scientific Research.

SIR ROY HARROD, F.B.A. and recipient of numerous academic honours, was the principal tutor in economics at Christ Church, Oxford, from 1923 until 1967. During the Second World War he served full-time in Winston Churchill's private statistical section 1940–2, and subsequently in an advisory capacity. He is a Vice-President of the Royal Economic Society, having served as President 1962–4, and was Joint Editor of the *Economic Journal* 1945–61. He has published eighteen books, of which many have been translated into foreign languages, and numerous contributions to learned journals in a number of centres.

K. WILLIAM KAPP is a Professor of Economics at the University of Basel, Switzerland. He has also taught at New York, Columbia and Wesleyan Universities, and at Brooklyn College, C.U.N.Y. His publications include *Social Costs of Private Enterprise, Toward a Science of Man in Society, Environmental Policies* and *Development Planning in Contemporary China and Other Essays,* and numerous articles dealing with social costs, environmental policies and the economics of underdevelopment.

HARVEY LEIBENSTEIN is Andelot Professor of Economics and Population at Harvard University, Cambridge in the United States. He has published on population theory, economic development, and the relation between microeconomic theory and organisation. His current research is on: (1) microeconomic approaches to the explanation of human fertility; and (2) the reformulation of microeconomic theory on the basis of psychological and unit postulates which differ from the conventional ones. The result of his recent research has appeared under the title *Beyond Economic Man*.

GUNNAR MYRDAL founded and directed the Institute for International Economic Studies in Stockholm. He is at present chairman of the board of two new research institutions: the Stockholm International Peace Research Institute (SIPRI) and the Latin American Institute. He is also the author of *Asian Drama: An Inquiry into the Poverty of Nations, Objectivity in Social Research, The Challenge of World Poverty* and *An American Dilemma*. He was awarded the Nobel Prize for Economics in 1974.

JAN TINBERGEN has been Professor of Economics at the Netherlands School of Economics since 1933. He has advised various governments and international organisations on economic matters, and is holder of honorary degrees from sixteen universities. His many publications include *Economic Policy, Principles and Design* and *Shaping the World Economy*. He was awarded the Nobel Prize for Economics in 1969.

SHIGETO TSURU is Emeritus Professor of Economics at Hitotsubashi University, Tokyo as well as being President; he is also Vice-President of the International Social Science Council. He has held visiting posts at many well-known American universities. His publications in English include *Essays on Marxian Economics, Essays on the Japanese Economy* and *Essays on Economic Development*. He has also been the editor of *Has Capitalism Changed?* and *Environmental Disruption – A Challenge to Social Scientists*. In his own language he has written extensively on the Japanese economy besides offering many contributions to professional journals.

Part One

A Framework

1 Introduction: Towards a New Paradigm*

Kurt Dopfer

> Time Present and Time Past
> are both perhaps Present in Time Future,
> and Time Future contained in Time Past.
> T. S. Eliott, *Four Quartets.*

I Purpose of the Book

Economics has always been in a crisis since it broke away from social philosophy in the late eighteenth century. But from time to time this crisis has been particularly acute. Such was the case at the turn of the last century when the classical predictions proved less and less true and, in response, the marginalist schools emerged. Such also was the case at the beginning of the 1930s when the proof of the established harmony propounded in that theory was contradicted by the Great Depression, giving rise to the new macroeconomics pioneered by Keynes. There is no

* I gratefully acknowledge comments and suggestions by Professors Takao Fukuchi, Takuma Yasui, S. D. B. Picken and Mr Mitsuo Sasaki. I owe a particular token of gratitude to Mr Lee E. Edlefsen who supported the project in many ways and also made useful comments on my essay. The responsibility for any remaining errors is my own.

doubt that contemporary economics is in a crisis, at least if crisis is defined as the inability to meet the challenge of the times. Problems like mass poverty, unbalanced affluence, increasing regional economic disparities, imbalances in population development, irrational disposition of non-renewable resources, and production and consumption processes ill-adjusted to the limited carrying capacity of the environment are among many pressing problems awaiting solution by economists.

The purpose of this book is to bring together responses from leading economists to these problems. Given the vast subject-matter, it is only to be expected that the specific emphasis given to various approaches differs among the authors. In a way one is reminded of the old Buddhist parable of the six blind men who meet an elephant and who, after having carefully touched the object, cannot agree whether it is a tree trunk, a wall or a rattlesnake. However, despite the different emphases given to the subject-matter and the differences in the approaches suggested, there is apparent consensus that changes in the science of economics are called for if it is to respond to the problems of the future.

The purpose of this introduction is to provide a framework for placing, comparing and evaluating the ideas of the contributors. The framework is organised with a view to the question of the areas in which changes are likely to occur.

II The Nature of Changes

Changes and, as their result, progress, occur in science in two fundamentally different ways. Changes may refer to a hypothesis, a theory, or a whole corpus of interrelated theories. Changes then occur when a hypothesis is contradicted by the facts by way of empirical testing, and, subsequently, is rejected and replaced by a new one. There are, however, other more fundamental changes which occur outside the conventional process of acquiring scientific knowledge. Such changes refer to the whole underlying structure of the scientific process, the kind of questions considered to be relevant for a science, the qualifications to its answers, the body of methods and techniques for testing of theories, the commonly consented degree of rigour required when accepting or rejecting theories, the institutional setting in which the researchers operate – in short, the whole set of factors which Kuhn combines in the notion 'paradigm'.[1] A change may occur when the ruling paradigm proves to be inadequate as a starting point for relevant questions and for the formulation and testing of theories. Such 'paradigm shift' does not obey the usual testing procedure as propounded by Popperian logic; falsification and verification are never directed to the paradigm itself. It is, therefore, conceivable that, in a science over long periods of time, the peculiar situation may prevail where 'scientific progress' occurs within an inadequate paradigm.

We may now restate the question asking whether the future changes in the discipline of economics will constitute a paradigm shift. Is the current paradigm a basis which calls forth the right kind of questions, allows for the formulation of relevant theories, suggests an appropriate degree of empirical testing, and, ultimately, proposes meaningful solutions to the most pressing problems of the future? Before turning to these questions, we will consider the current paradigm of economics to which changes have to be related.

III The Current Paradigm

It may be generally agreed upon, and Tsuru states it explicitly (see Chapter 7), that the current paradigm is largely constituted by what is called 'neoclassical theory'. The central object of investigation within this paradigm is the *market*. Institutionally, the market is conceived as being composed of many individuals – the 'atoms' – who enter the market scene either as consumers or producers. Their activities are confined, as Leibenstein accurately observes (see Chapter 3), to activities within the market context, precluding economically relevant activities in non-market contexts. The explanation of their behaviour rests entirely on the assumption that they will try to *maximise* their *own satisfactions*, and, in pursuing these, will behave *rationally*. These behavioural assumptions have never been specified analytically in their psychological and sociological complexity nor have they been subject to empirical scrutiny. Their roots can be traced back, as Myrdal recalls (see Chapter 5), to the philosophy of utilitarianism and the hedonistic associational psychology of the eighteenth and nineteenth centuries.

The economic problem with which the individual is typically confronted is to make a 'best' *choice among given alternatives.*[2] The basic conditions under which the maximising individual operates are exogenously determined and do not change in the model; production and utility functions are stable, and so is the distribution of income and wealth. Assuming two well-behaved production functions in the form

$$A = f^a(K, L)$$

and $$B = f^b(K, L),$$

the problem of maximisation can be defined as

maximise $$B = f^b(K, L)$$

subject to $$A_o - f^a(K, L) = 0,$$

where A_o can be any value of A.

If the conditions for maximisation are satisfied, the efficient allocation of resources is secured independent of the quantity or the price of K or L. It applies, for example, equally to less-developed as well as to developed countries. It is, in fact, the universal application of this principle which – as some neoclassical economists suggest – make economics an 'objective' discipline.[3]

Indeed, most of what follows are derivations from this principle. A description of all points of efficient resource allocations within a given resource endowment is derived from a large number of simple propositions about efficient allocative alternatives. Similar to the locus of efficient allocations, a functional relationship between the outputs themselves can be derived, and a set of 'best' alternatives of relevant outputs defined. The production-possibility frontier being the locus of all solutions to the maximisation problem, the only question left is to define the optimal set among a multitude of efficient sets. Here, the consumer – the closing link in the model – comes in; as per usual he acts as a rational maximiser. Applying the Lagrangean multiplier and using the calculus for solving the problems, the analysis leads to the conclusion that, with given technology and input endowments, the marginal rate of transformation on the production-possibility frontier shows how individuals have to exchange one good for another, and that the optimal set is obtained when the marginal rate of transformation equals the marginal rate of substitution – in the language of plain geometry, a point of tangency between production-possibility and indifference curves.

The result can easily be extended to situations with a large number of individuals. The consistency of the propositions in the context of *general equilibrium theory* is secured by the assumptions of perfect competition, with no externalities, informational transparency, no informational costs, and so on. The individuals placed into this environment will continuously adjust their patterns of production, and will exchange the commodities they have produced, until all have identical marginal rates of substitution. Prices serve as indicators of common value, and make the rates of substitution between the different alternatives comparable. Any non-equilibrium position of the system allows the individuals to gain. Being maximisers they will take advantage of potential gains until all are used up. Having thus reached equilibrium, that is having fulfilled the equilibrium condition,

$$Q_{di} - Q_{si} = 0, \qquad i = 1, \ldots, n,$$

where Q stands for quantity, the subscripts d and s for the amount demanded and supplied, and n for the number of commodities, the state of the system is called *Pareto optimal.* At a Pareto-optimal state there is no change that will benefit some people without making others worse off. The optimum solution, of course, does not say anything about, say, the optimal state of the exogenous variables, such as technology, natural resources, population, and so on, or about the desirability of a given wealth and income structure; nor does it include an ethical valuation of the consumer choice. Clearly there is a wide range of possible Pareto-optimal solutions.

The theoretical limitations of the approach are usually stated in an explicit manner. In fact the limitations themselves provide the decisive stimuli to maintain further theoretical explorations and to legitimate further refinement of the model. The limitations of the approach, however, have had no adverse effect, whatsoever, on the current paradigm; in those cases where its limitations are quoted as proof of the irrelevancy of the whole theory, the contradicting propositions can easily be treated as interesting 'deviant' opinions which serve more as an opportunity for proving intellectual tolerance (by adding a respectful footnote) than for initiating research along those lines. This is true for the neoclassical theory as the paradigm proper, be it the branch of partial market equilibrium theory, comparative statics, dynamics, or the neoclassical theory of economic growth. But the 'classical orthodoxy' is equally present, though less apparent, in Keynes's *General Theory* since Keynes only argued that the 'classical' system 'broke down' with regard to its determination of the aggregate 'volume' and not with regard to its 'direction' of employment and production. As far as resource allocation and distribution were concerned the system remained undetermined if regress was not made to 'classical' theory.[4]

The brief sketch of the current neoclassical paradigm is necessarily a rough generalisation. However, those who have advanced the most refinement of the models probably would admit that the sketch is essentially correct. Let me stress the essential features once more. Theories based on the current paradigm

(i) describe the behaviour of economic agents in the marketplace within

(ii) a time horizon relevant for the outcomes of these individuals, typically of a short- or medium-term nature;

(iii) they rely on behavioural assumptions such as exclusive self-interest, rationality and a maximisation drive which have not been specified analytically in their psychological and sociological nature nor rigorously subjected to empirical testing;

(iv) focusing on short-run behavioural and flow variables, the theories define the equilibrium of the system consequently as a state of rest of these short-run variables; variables such as population, natural resources and technology which affect the functioning of the system in the long run are being kept constant when describing the move of the system towards equilibrium or its final equilibrium state, leaving undefined the long-run equilibrium position of the system;

(v) given the static determination of the system, choices are restricted to relative choices within given alternatives; and

(vi) the resulting optima share the limitations of the assumptions and variables from which they are derived. They inherit normative biases, particularly with regard to the preferences of present generations over past generations, the goals of production over goals of distribution, and market activities over non-market (government) activities.

Having thus defined the current paradigm, an assessment of changes such as a paradigm shift depends on the delineation of the future development of economics. This requires some clarification. Do we describe where economics 'ought' to go, or do we simply 'predict'? Since this essay refers to the contributions contained in the book, the question calls for an assessment of the contributions in terms of the 'normative versus predictive' scenario. If not an impossible task, this assessment implies at least an unacceptable degree of arbitrariness. Therefore, I will not attempt this. However, the book bears witness that agreement on the major problem issues can be reached; it is conceivable that statements about which theories *ought* to be applied may converge with theories which *will* be applied.

As for this essay I will deliberately focus on the issue of where economics in the future *ought* to go rather than where economics *will* go. This in itself may determine the selection of the references I will make to the various contributions.

The ideas are grouped around four propositions. They are respectively concerned with a holistic approach, a long-run view in economics, economics as an empirical science, and economics as political economy.

IV Proposition 1: The Need for a Holistic Approach

First, consider the problem of the proper *scope of empirical observation.* Ever since Darwin, scientists, including social scientists, have understood that every entity is a component of a structure which itself is a component of a related lower or higher structure. From this premise quite naturally evolved the concept of the *environment* as a complex web defining the nature and relatedness of these components and structures. Darwinism, of course, was quite popular in economics some time ago. But even at that time the compartmentalisation of the sciences was so far advanced that Darwin's original concept of the environment was distorted into Social Darwinism.[5] Though it is difficult to recover from this fall in esteem and to theoretical meaninglessness Darwin's basic concept of the environment has to be re-introduced to all socially relevant sciences, including economics, in order to provide a breadth of empirical observation which allows the perception of problems in their complexity and the relating of single phenomena to each other in their proper quality of interdependency.[6]

The basic theoretical approach derived from an 'environmental' observation of reality is *holism* (see Chapter 5), which is yet another theory the modern form of which dates back to the year 1926. Holism as developed by Smuts and later by Bews states that, as a consequence of the existence of a complex environment, all phenomena have to be analysed in the context of this environment.[7]

This typically calls for *interdisciplinary* research. However, interdisciplinary research pursued in a holistic manner has some features which distinguishes it from the traditional concept of interdisciplinary research. The traditional procedure has been to perceive an economic phenomenon, say $\mathscr{E}$, to formulate the relevant questions in terms of economics, E, to choose the specific scientific ingredients such as available economic theories, methods and data, *e*. Then allowance may be made for some non-economic phenomena, ξ, to be included as additional explanatory variables whenever a gap in the model suggests that this is necessary. This approach constitutes progress over the alternative traditional approach which excludes non-economic variables from economic models and refers them back to the discipline to which they belong. But as it has been aptly put, the chap in the other discipline 'isn't there'.[8] Interdisciplinary research emerging from a holistic view perceives the economic phenomena, $\mathscr{E}'$, within the over-all context of which this phenomenon constitutes part, say $\mathscr{E}'$, related to phenomena $\xi', \ldots \gamma', \mu'$. Based on this holistic perspective the relevant question for economics, E', is asked, and the choice of relevant theories, methods, and data from the science of economics as well as from other sciences is made. This clearly is a difficult task. It calls for a basic understanding of relevant non-economic disciplines, and for the ability to integrate and not merely to analyse. Though challenging, the task is not impossible. The increasing number of conferences with interdisciplinary orientation indicates a movement in this direction. The results of these meetings will depend on the awareness of the need to substitute holistic interdisciplinary research for the narrow approach.

Thus encircled, the proper view of an economist's reality plus the concept of environmental perception and the idea that research should be conducted in a holistic manner, *system analysis* as a unified methodology and theory comes into focus.[9] However, as the perception of economic phenomena became narrowed in the subdisciplines of economics, the perception of the over-all economic system correspondingly narrowed. The classical writers had a comprehensive view of the economic system. They analysed both the aspects of positive and negative feedbacks, and automatic and controlled feedbacks. In contemporary systems analysis the former is, by and large, excluded. The development of the system is supposed to be determined by positive feedbacks (for example investment) and not by negative feedbacks which would bring the system back into a long-run equilibrium position.[10] The economic system is therefore understood as an 'open' system as opposed to the classical notion of the 'closed' system where negative feedbacks force it into a long-run equilibrium position.[11] However, the emergence of disturbing effects which stem from exponentially growing entropic processes, that is the dispersion of energy and natural resources under conditions of absolute scarcity and ecological limitations, suggest that a shift from an 'open' to a 'closed' economic system is again to be expected.

From an over-all view of the system, the economic system becomes a *sub-system* which relates to other sub-systems, and has to be assessed in an over-all context which explains the interactions between the various sub-systems.[12]

Consider a few examples which show how the economic system is related in cause and effect to other sub-systems, and how this will produce repercussions for the scope of economics. The *Keynesian* system, for example, holds as its basic proposition that an aggregate of partial market equilibria would not necessarily correspond to a full use of the over-all capacity of an economy. The postulate derived from this has been that the government should be allowed to decide upon the volume of aggregate demand to secure the full use of the over-all capacity of the economy. In the context of a holistic system approach, however, such a postulate may conflict with postulates which relate to the functioning of other sub-systems. For example, higher aggregate demand, though leading to higher output and employment, may simultaneously lead to an increase in the depletion of energy and non-renewable resources as it may aggravate the ecological imbalance.

Other examples can be provided on a more disaggregated, that is sectoral basis. For the complex interdependence between the *agricultural* sector as part of the *economic* system and the agricultural sector as part of the *biological* system, Kapp's contribution (Chapter 6) provides some thoughts. It is clear from that analysis that the treatment of the agricultural system as a merely economic system subject to biological 'restrictions' yields a result biased towards the maximisation of outputs measured in economic terms as against the realisation of objectives, ecological and biological ones, not allowed for in economic calculus. The result, a disrupted equilibrium of non-economic systems and an economic system threatened in its functioning, calls for a *system-wide*, to borrow Kapp's term, assessment of agricultural activities. By its very nature this is a holistic system approach.

There are similar cases of a system-wide interrelatedness in the *industrial* sector. A major link goes from technology and capital accumulation to the depletion of non-renewable resources and the impairment of the ecological equilibrium. The research problems, however, are not limited to the analysis of the detrimental effects of the economic system on other systems. As Tinbergen has pointed out elsewhere,[13] the major challenge will be to define processes of capital accumulation where additional application of technology does *not* lead to the depletion of non-renewable resources but rather these resources are saved and possibly substituted by renewable resources due to a proper response of technology. The question is one of analysis and one of formulating alternatives.

V Proposition 2: The Need for a Long-Run View in Economics

The distinction between the short- and the long-run view lends itself to the classification of research areas. By definition, a *short*-run view will be applied in analysing phenomena which change quickly. Business cycles, for example, or behaviour in the general equilibrium context is of this nature. On the other hand, a *long*-run view will be applied when the behaviour of variables which change slowly is analysed. Variables treated in conventional analysis as constants, such as natural-resource conditions, population, technology, environmental-carrying capacity and institutional factors are of this nature. The research choice for a specific class of variables, however, does not in all cases determine the time horizon to be applied in that analysis. For instance, the analysis of consumer behaviour is amenable to both short- and long-run views as is the analysis of aggregate magnitudes, supply factors and institutions. Our proposition should be understood that a shift towards a long-run view will occur with regard to both, variables thus far analysed in their short-run behaviour, and variables thus far not analysed in their dynamic behaviour at all.

Long-run variables may be classified into supply, demand and institutional variables. The analytical task is to describe changes in these variables. These changes may refer to the past describing a historical sequence, or to the future, predicting the time path of the present epoch. Future changes of the variables are based on the past, both in analysis and reality. Time is *historical* time. It cannot be simply treated as a continuous variable which takes any value ranging from minus infinity to plus infinity. To treat the actual present as 'accumulated past' is not feasible without reference to a historical point if statements about changes are to be made. It seems to be a common conviction in current economics that 'economic laws' can be found which can be applied to all historical instances, and that something like a 'formal history' can exist. As a result, it has frequently been demanded that economic history be banned from the curriculum as has been done in the case of physics.[14] However, in the social sciences, phenomena cannot be reduced to abstract categories applicable in all time and space instances as in some types of physics. The ahistorical nature of the current concepts can be directly linked to the analytical emphasis given to short-run variables which change only in the *status quo.* If economics would deal only with these variables it might, indeed, be a 'formal' science. The economic system being at present in a crucial transitional state which demands 'historical' explanation, reliance on such formal treatment is counter-productive. Long-run variables lend themselves to meaningful theoretical generalisation only when reference is made to a particular historical *epoch* or a sequence of them. If there is a *general* theory of socio-economic development, it is the generalisation of all historical experience.

It will be remembered that the long-run variables are confined to the limiting conditions of a 'closed' system, and that they are to move on a time path converging towards a long-run equilibrium position. Supply, demand, and institutional variables have to be assessed under these historical conditions.

As for the *supply* variables, Tinbergen proposed recently to distinguish between exhaustibles and non-exhaustibles when classifying the types of natural production factors, activities and products.[15] Exhaustible resources are materials supplied by the earth and the atmosphere; they are in finite quantities available as reserves. Non-exhaustible resources are such production factors as solar-radiation energy, human capital, or technological progress. Writing for the annual production of exhaustible activities $\dot{y}$, for the total stock accumulated since the beginning of production y, for the initial stock available A, for the actual production of non-exhaustibles x, and for the total annual production z, we have

$$z = x + \dot{y}.$$

This distinction between x and $\dot{y}$ depends entirely on the criterion of long-run availability of the production factors. While x may fit into a traditional Cobb–Douglas production function, $\dot{y}$ has to be determined according to A and y. y is given at any time t as a quantity y_t, the quantity of exhaustibles used up already. A is given by the total stock of exhaustible resources on the earth. Various production functions for $\dot{y}$ can be assumed. Their precise shape depends on their empirical evaluation. In a first approach where A is assumed to be given and known, Tinbergen proposes a production function in the form,

$$\dot{y} = \delta(A - y)y,$$

leading to the development over time for y in the form of a logistic curve, and for $\dot{y}$ in a bell-shaped curve. Other production functions can be chosen, for example a quasi-logistic or goniometric function. Though the search for the best fit of these functions with the empirical data or projections is crucial for a theoretical 'fine-tuning', the novelty of the approach lies in the exposition of a theoretical structure which brings home the classical production factor of 'land'. Once this theoretical distinction is accepted, the present knowledge of the historical conditions dictate that we distinguish between x and $\dot{y}$ in the production function which is to be applied at present. Having reached this point, theoretical statements about A and y have to be made suggesting, for the formulation of a theory, a time span ranging from early industrialisation to hundred years and more into the future. This will call for empirical research along the lines of long-run variables untouched by present economics because they are 'given', not only as the assumptions in theory, but also as presumably inexhaustible resources in reality.

The proposition that *capital accumulation* cannot go on for ever on an exponential path since the ecosystem is limited has been frequently made and has a high intuitive appeal. A theoretical generalisation of the causal interconnections between the capital-accumulation process and the related historical–environmental factors is still very much in the dark. On the one hand, explanatory variables underlying the capital-accumulation process within a specific economic system, say a capitalist market system, have to be determined; this amounts to the enormous intellectual task of formulating a theory of (post-) capitalist economic development, say in the Marxian or Schumpeterian sense. On the other hand, explanatory variables of the capital-accumulation process have to be related to explanatory variables of corresponding co-systems.[16]

The analytical emphasis given to capital accumulation has been leading to erroneous conclusions with regard to the *transferability* and *validity* of the models when applied to *different historical situations.* An analytical reduction of the economic-development process to a process of capital accumulation may perhaps do some justice to early European industrialisation experience. If on the basis of such a model a telescoping of European experience to less-developed countries is assumed to be feasible, the analysis must end in an impasse. Approximately, this is what happened in the capital-focused phase of development theory up to the 1960s.[17] Capital accumulation (in its broadest sense) depends on specific historical conditions, and as long as these conditions are not provided this process cannot occur. Economic development is to be understood as a historical phenomenon, and the explanation of its 'conditional' explanatory variables is likely to be crucial for the validity of the theory.

Finally, consider *population*. Being both a supply and demand variable it plays a dual role. This is not so in contemporary neoclassical growth theory where population is treated as an exogenously determining supply variable, and not as a demand variable. This is merely a specific instance of the general neglect of the demand side in neoclassical theory. Demand, however, becomes a constituent variable if the rate of growth of population is high as compared to the rate of growth of the total gross national product. This is particularly evident in the less-developed countries where (under supply conditions insufficient to absorb population increases productively) additional demand due to population increases leads to a drop in the growth rates of *per capita* incomes, and hampers the initiation or sustaining of desirable development processes.[18] Furthermore, population as a demand variable comes in when long-run supply constraints have to be considered. As far as non-renewable resources and environmental constraints are the determinants of demand limitations, the case will apply first, and above all, to developed countries where the use of these supply factors is large and the marginal utility of increases in consumer demand is low when compared to less-developed countries. The neoclassical proposition – that, in the steady state, a country with a growth rate of population which is one per cent higher than another country will also have a growth rate of total output one per cent higher than that country – does not hold once the model is applied to a historical situation where other long-run variables play a crucial role as explanatory variables.

VI Proposition 3: The Need to View Economics as an Empirical Science

The standard rule for scientific inquiry states that (1) a theory has to be formulated, and (2) the theory has to be tested against the empirical facts so that it be either verified or falsified.

Theoretical propositions may be stated in a general form, for example that there is a relationship between A and B, such that $A = f(B)$, or they may be specific stating that there is a relationship between A and B, say in the form of a linear relationship. If the empirical testing contradicts a specific proposition, the basic assumptions of the theory are likely to remain intact. The theory as amended in the light of newly acquired facts and predictions derived from the improved theory is again subjected to empirical testing. The 'circular' reasoning, however, can be interrupted when empirical evidence suggests a rejection of general assumptions or hypotheses. In the above example the assumptions state that the relevant variables be A and B and that the relationship is $B \rightarrow A$. (Assuming that $A = f(B)$, indeed, a causal interpretation can be given.) This proposition can be rejected by stating that either the relationship is a different one, for example $A \rightarrow B$, or the choice of the explanatory variables is inappropriate – the latter being the more probable and frequent case. The inappropriateness in the choice of variables may be due to the fact that the theory includes as explanatory variables only A and B while C also might be relevant for a theory which is to have satisfactory predictive power, or the choice of variables may prove to be inappropriate because A and B are not relevant while C and D are. While in the former case the theory usually is extended by introducing new relevant variables, for example C, in the latter case a whole set of new variables, definitions and hypotheses will be required. In both instances, but particularly in the latter, the earlier empirical-testing procedure and the results thus derived cannot provide sufficient help for reformulating the general theoretical propositions since it is determined in scope and direction by these original 'false' propositions. If, say, A and B but not C are considered to be relevant, there will be little empirical research on C or the interrelationships between A, B and C. Alternatively, C and D are relevant explanatory variables but A and B are not; previous empirical research on A and B cannot serve adequately as an empirical starting point for the formulating of adequate theories. Methodologically, the broadening or erection of a general theoretical framework may distinctively differ from the continuous theorising and empirical testing within the established framework. Testing within the framework set by the assumptions can rely on rigorous methods of quantification and estimation while the search for new assumptions calls forth the intellectual capacity to make generalisations about a segment of reality which is yet theoretically undefined, unclassified and unexplained, and which is empirically unexplored, at best relying on 'facts without theory'. Proposition 3 can be understood to mean that the empirical re-orientation of economics shall not only be directed towards enhanced scrutiny of *existing theories* and a 'fine-tuning' within an *established set of assumptions* (which will include the reformulation of theories to make them testable), but also that it shall include the observation and evaluation of a broader range of empirical facts which serve as a basis for the formulation of *new assumptions* and *new theories*.

Drawing the usual (although not unambiguous) distinction between *positive* and *normative* economics, empirical research is at home – following a widely accepted view – in positive economics. Positive statements explain the 'facts as they are', and the adequacy of a theory can thus be tested by an appeal to the facts. On the contrary, normative economics explains what 'should be' referring to a scale which includes value judgements as well as the facts. It is assumed that such theory cannot be founded on an empirical basis and the validity of the theoretical propositions cannot be tested by a mere appeal to facts. Once this view is accepted the possibility of arriving at a general welfare theory then depends on the degree to which empirical facts can be dismissed without entire loss of relevance, and also on the degree to which the propositions can be formalised. Thus, the basic propositions of contemporary welfare theory consist of criteria for general performance-satisfactoriness (that is Pareto-satisfactoriness) and a set of marginal equivalences – both, ahistorical, untestable and irrefutable. Proposition 3 should be understood to mean that, besides the area proper of empirical research and theory testing, the area of normative economics will also have to be given a more solid empirical foundation if this branch of economics is to be further developed so as to arrive at meaningful theoretical statements.

As for *positive economics*, enhanced empirical relevance will prove to be critical; (1) for the formulation of more valid assumptions and (2) for a proper assessment of the economic system under new 'environmental' conditions.

In current mainstream economics, the *assumptions* are based on hypothetical behaviour (the intellectual roots of which were mentioned in Section III on 'The Current Paradigm') and not on actual (empirically observed) behaviour. This hypothetical behaviour, in addition, is reduced in the assumptions to 'ideal' behaviour, for example, as Leibenstein points out, the logic of optimisation serves as a vehicle for describing actual behaviour.

Given this twofold reduction in the assumptions, traditional economic theory has been able to avoid an empirical enquiry into the behaviour of economic agents and the institutions in which they behave. Having narrowed the empirical scope, further development of the theory was blocked at an early and most crucial stage, that is at the stage of the formulating of assumptions.

Specifically, with a view to the theory of economic development, most economists would agree that a better understanding of institutions and behaviour is critical for a theory which tries to explain the *dynamic* aspects of economic development. If the theory restricts itself to describing a static economy, where major changes in institutions and behaviour do not occur, the conceptual and cognitive limitations to a resource framework may not interfere with the search for a valid theory. If, however, the theory intends to describe *transitional* processes, for example the transition from an agrarian to a dualistic economy, and its determining causation processes (the causation of agricultural innovation, diffusion of innovations, or surplus generating behaviour), then an explanation of institutions and behaviour is necessary for the validity of such theory.[19]

The second problem area refers to the *economic macro system* and its complex interactions with other systems. The specific need for empirical research springs immediately to mind when we visualise some of the contemporary disaster areas. Data on output of waste, repercussions of waste disposal on the ecological balance, urban disamenities, congestion phenomena, or data on pollution damage, are grossly lacking. Additional empirical data on these problem issues are likely to have immediate political impact. A comprehensive theoretical and ultimately political apprehension of these data, however, is only possible within a theoretical and methodological framework which shows the interdependencies of the data. Theoretically, such research may emphasise flow and stock relationships, and, therefore, methodologically favour a concept which shows the interrelatedness of such data. Tinbergen (Chapter 2) mentions various alternatives, among them an extension of the input–output table which now would include empirical data from various systems (not only from the economic system). Kapp (Chapter 6) and Myrdal (Chapter 5) stress the 'system-wide' complexity and causal interrelatedness of flow and stock variables, and, therefore, suggest a holistic system approach as an adequate methodological device. As for the need for empirical research, a 'system-wide' account propounded in both views will encounter an empirical 'no-man's land', or, in terms of our introductory exposé, there is likely to be a significant number of *C* and *D* variables on which empirical knowledge is grossly lacking. Since many of the new explanatory variables lie outside the area of economics proper, such empirical research is, by its very nature, *interdisciplinary*.

As for *normative economics*, the proposition to extend the empirical basis runs against much that is sacred. Following the doctrine, utilities cannot (and have not to) be compared between people. Consequently, the total welfare of a community is not defined as the sum of individual utilities, but as a *vector.*[20] If the maximum welfare of a community is to be defined, a criterion to evaluate different vectors has to be introduced. Choosing, for example, as a criterion for the ordering of vectors Pareto-optimum conditions, a utility vector can be said to be preferable to another utility vector when at least one of its components is greater than the corresponding component of the other vector, and none is less. The ordering criterion is by no means a substitute for a social-welfare function which would have to show how individual utilities are to be 'added up'. If the question to be settled is not merely whether vector **A** is desirable to vector **B** but how much **A** is desirable to **B**, a method of measurement and a measuring scale has to be agreed upon which can, following the doctrine, be found only in the realm of ethical beliefs.[21] The assumptions of contemporary welfare theory, consumer sovereignty, or a democratic passing from individual to social preferences, are axiomatic. They are simply 'good', and are thus 'desirable'. To state how much they are 'good' and 'desirable' would mean, again, to make an inadmissible value judgement. Similarly, nothing is said whether the assumptions have any material meaning in a given historical context, or whether they are 'empirically feasible'. If a passing from individual to social preferences is not feasible, it is because the axioms are logically incompatible.[22] There is no criterion for the 'choice of axioms' since the empirical dimension is reduced to the mere stating of the axioms. If a choice is made, it is assumed to have to rely exclusively upon value judgements, not on the historical situation. In short, there is a tendency in modern welfare theory to overrate the differences in psychological satisfactions *and* the relevance of ethical beliefs while neglecting the empirical determination of these. Thus, modern welfare economics is (i) empirically void when it comes to defining states of social welfare, and (ii) provides little criteria for optimally or 'reasonably' implementing a social-welfare function. The proposition to give welfare theory empirical relevance (beyond an axiomatic treatment) will meet the objection that this can be done only by introducing value judgements which inadmissibly blur the objectivity of the theory. The brief sketch of an *empirical welfare theory* shall indicate that it is not necessary to let the 'best' become the enemy of the 'good'.

A first empirical account is necessary to define the areas in which it is permissible (*a*) to apply concepts like 'individual taste', 'psychological satisfaction', and 'value judgement' as 'choice parameters', and (*b*) to conceive the choices as exchanges of one utility for an alternative utility on the locus of an indifference curve. Given the two criteria, a delineation of the two areas require that we distinguish between (i) utilities to which (*a*) and (*b*) apply and (ii) utilities to which (*a*) and (*b*) do not apply. The classification itself suggests that the propositions of modern welfare theory are plausible for the areas (i) and (ii) only to various degrees. Thus, the proposition that utilities are, for example, not interpersonally comparable must be regarded as an unnecessary general proposition since it can be specified by distinguishing between areas of utilities. The problem, then, is to establish operational criteria which allow a classification of the areas (i) and (ii). Again, the prevalent view holds (mainly for the sake of consistency of the theory) that (*a*) and (*b*) are equally applicable for all conceivable instances (with a few exceptions), which is an implausible proposition. There is ample empirical evidence to suggest that, say, 'psychological satisfaction' or 'taste' as 'choice parameters' are of marginal importance as compared to other parameters relevant for determining utility. The general reliance on a basically hedonist 'choice parameter' is theoretically impermissible. There are likely to be considerable repercussions on the acceptability of the conclusions derived from modern welfare theory once the empirical limitation, or 'historical' nature, of this 'choice parameter' has been quite understood.

In this basic attempt to set up empirical categories of utilities and corresponding 'choice parameters' suffice it to draw a distinction between utilities which can be satisfied by (I) individual goods, and (II) collective goods. Similarly, suffice to distinguish within these categories between (*A*) 'subsistence utility' and (*B*) 'supplementary utility' (above subsistence level).

Utilities (I/A) obviously do *not* depend on 'taste' or 'value judgement'. Utility is determined here by its 'biological quality' to enable life. There is, though, a 'variable' part since psychological satisfaction derived from life may differ. Some people may also prefer the composition of diet X to that of diet Y (although such choice rarely is visualised by people in reality). The conclusion that nothing can be said empirically about utility because the 'variable' part is determined by subjective factors, and is thus not interpersonally comparable, means committing a gross *pars pro toto* fallacy since utility is almost exclusively determined by the part attributable to 'survival utility'. Once an absolute priority of one utility over another is empirically plausible, the choice on the locus of indifference curves becomes unrealistic. Nobody wants to 'trade in' his life for any other good. It is, therefore, reasonable to make the theoretical generalisation that people impose a *lexical* ordering on their choice of utilities,[23] that is, people wish that A be fully satisfied before B. It follows that the transformation from individual to social welfare is not dependent on an arbitrary ethical judgement but on the lexical ordering of utilities whose existence and content can be objectively determined. A social-welfare state (S_A) can be said to be preferable to a social-welfare state (S_B) if a larger *fraction* of the population in $A(P_a)$ than in $B(P_b)$ has satisfied 'survival utility' (U^s); thus, $U^s_A > U^s_B$ whenever $P_a > P_b$, and imposing a lexical ordering on the utilities, $S_A > S_B$, whenever $U^s_A > U^s_B$. The objection that one man's 'supplementary utility' might possibly be higher than another man's 'survival utility', and that, therefore, the lexical ordering itself implies an arbitrary (objectively not defensible) value judgement, is sophistry for which a proper place in theology should be found. As for economics, little is lost for the validity of a general theory of welfare if we work with the assumption that the life of one man has a higher utility than any other welfare category of another man, and that this is true for all men. Familiar propositions of welfare theory need revision in the light of the 'new' assumptions. To take a case in point, Pareto-optimality is not generally acceptable any more, because we can say that it is a good thing to make a person better off if it contributes to his survival even if it makes another person worse off as long as it does not affect the other person's survival.

Contemporary welfare theory does not provide a basis for empirical research. Its propositions cannot be subjected to empirical testing, and further development of the theory is not considered to depend on newly acquired facts. It is of little surprise, therefore, that we encounter a situation where we have a logically consistent theory entirely unrelated to empirical results. For the beginning, there are enough empirical results to substantiate the theoretical framework outlined above. There is a substantial body of cross-country studies on 'social indicators'.[24] There is agreement that some utilities are to be treated as 'absolute necessities' which have lexical priority over others. The anonymous acceptance of standards on 'minimum requirements' (for example for food) and 'minimum living standard' (for example for health, clothing, footwear and shelter) on a national and international scale (United Nations) suggests that there is actual agreement on the lexical ordering for some utilities.[25]

As for *utilities* (II/*A*), empirical evidence suggests that an empirical ordering of utilities and its transformation to an 'objective' (scientifically agreed) empirical social-welfare function is equally possible. *Collective goods* to which 'subsistence utility' is attached include 'environmental commodities' such as land, water and air. 'Minimum standards' are currently being developed by natural scientists, biologists and technologists, enabling the definition and empirical determination of environmental subsistence utilities.[26] Modern welfare theory includes in the utility function only 'economic goods' implying that resources have to be expended on it to contribute to welfare. Since environmental subsistence utilities did thus far not require any resources to be expended on it the good was 'free' and not a determinant of welfare. It is one of the paradoxes of welfare economics (although easily predictable from its formal nature) that the environmental utilities become relevant as variables of a welfare function at a time when they actually contribute less to welfare. Collective subsistence utilities and supplementary utilities are of an entirely different nature. Supplementary utilities are derived from the consumption of commodities like public parks, police protection or television sets. They are structurally unrelated, exchangeable and, to some extent, marginally variable. To the contrary, collective subsistence utilities share none of these features. The respective commodities are (i) not divisible into unrelated components nor are they marginally variable but they constitute part of a complex structure which functionally and causally relates the individual components to each other, and (ii) they are not exchangeable for alternative commodities along indifference curves but have an absolute priority which commands lexical ordering. From (i) it follows that utility from an environmental commodity can be derived (*a*) in its quality as a single component, say as the commodity of air or water – α utility – and (*b*) in its quality as a structured entity and as a causally interacting part of the whole – *A-utility*. *α-utility* can be derived from a component only if all components provide *A utility* since each of the components constitutes an indispensable part for the quality of the whole. The degree of utility which a single component provides is therefore equal to the utility it provides to enable the whole system to work, and, if environmental minimum standards are applied to the utilities of single components, the utility of a single component is equal to the utility of the whole system since the absence of a minimum standard of the *A-utility* of any component will lead to a collapse of the whole system. In terms of logic we arrive at the paradoxical result that the value of a single component is equal to the value of the whole, and the value of the whole is equal to the value of the whole multiplied by the number of its components. The logic applicable to structured entities is not that of simple arithmetic. Irrespective of the formulation of a logically consistent evaluation procedure, the result indicates that the evaluation of the utility of a single component along lines of resource expenditures measured in opportunity costs for alternative utilities cannot provide any help for reasonably determining these utilities. This conclusion is confirmed by (ii). People impose a lexical ordering on *α-utilities* of all components, for reasons mentioned earlier. Independent of the contribution a single component makes to the whole, *α-utility* is given a lexical ordering over 'supplementary utilities'.

All assumptions on which modern welfare theory is built seem to indicate that *supplementary utilities* (*B*/I and *B*/II) are its domain proper. However, already a brief discussion will show that modern welfare theory will have to constitute an integral part of a whole new welfare theory rather than absorbing new parts in its extended framework. The central welfare component or utility variable of modern welfare theory is the *economic commodity*. While for some utility variables economic commodities can adequately serve as operational counterparts, for example for individual subsistence utilities, other utility variables cannot be expressed in terms of economic commodities but only in terms of (i) *non-economic commodities*, and (ii) non-commodities or *processes*. The hypothesis with regard to the future development is that (i) and (ii) will increase relative to economic commodities, and that this phenomenon will probably demand novel theoretical approaches as well as empirical research in areas which were traditionally across the borderline of the science of economics but are now gaining relevance for the proper assessment of welfare.

As *non-economic commodities* we include 'psychological satisfaction', or, in the original Pigouvian sense of welfare, the 'states of consciousness'. This can mean, first that the 'states of consciousness' and not the economic commodities are the utility variables proper, and second that the 'states of consciousness' are utility variables *sui generis* as distinct from economic commodities. As for the first meaning, it is sufficient to recall that modern welfare theory reduces the utility of an economic commodity in two ways. First, it considers as theoretically irrelevant whether a purchased good is actually consumed (thus the choice refers to the purchase of a good), and, secondly, it considers as irrelevant for the assessment of utility what psychological satisfaction a person actually derives from the purchase (or rather consumption) of an economic commodity. Various improvements are conceivable. As Leibenstein points out, the individual who makes the choice between commodities is frequently not the same individual who derives utility from the chosen commodity. Continuous indifference curves may not indicate an optimal choice (nor approximate actual behaviour) when the commodities are 'status goods' since psychological satisfaction is derived from a 'distinctive style' expressed in physically discontinuous 'bundles of status goods'. 'Psychological satisfaction' as a commodity *sui generis* can be defined as the 'psychological surplus value' which is attached to economic commodities and to other welfare entities by the society as a whole or by various classes, groups, or individuals of that society. If psychological satisfaction is derived from the consumption of a 'status good', it might be adequately expressed as 'complementary utility' of that economic commodity. If psychological satisfaction is derived from another welfare entity, it constitutes a commodity *sui generis* proper which should be included as an autonomous utility variable in a utility function since this utility does not appear in any economic commodity included in the utility function. Non-economic commodities providing utility are social acceptance, achievement, respect, and other psychological satisfactions an individual derives from his place or role in society due to the value system prevailing in that society.[27] This is of course strong beer for economists who declare as axiomatic that nothing about welfare can objectively be said beyond statements about conjectural choices among physically determined alternatives. Indeed, the task of making the concept operational is formidable. There are no prices (although money may serve as a *numéraire*), no exchange of commodities, no market, and therefore no market equilibrium with an explicitly determinable optimum quality. The possibility of arriving at adequate definitions and an operational concept which allows us to formulate a set of testable and refutable hypotheses will depend entirely on the possibility of successfully conducting *interdisciplinary* research. The fact that non-economic commodities are difficult to define and to empirically determine does not disprove their existence nor does it provide an indication of their minor relevance. In any case it is not fruitful to further develop welfare theory along the established lines, where human welfare is reduced to economic welfare, and economic welfare is reduced to a conjectural choice among economic commodities.

The intellectual task of assessing human welfare becomes more delicate when we include *collective* 'supplementary utilities' (*B*/II). While environmental aesthetics or urban amenities are difficult enough to assess, we have further to consider that collective supplementary utilities can be often enjoyed only together with individual utilities. The utility from a television set, U_s, and from television programme, U_p, is not $U_s + U_p$, but it is the utility derived from 'watching television', U_x. U_s and U_p are mutually indispensible for the utility of either. If one is absent the utility of the other is zero (excluding exchange for alternative commodities). The whole is more than the sum of its parts, that is $U_x > U_s + U_p$. This concept applied to a gradual assessment of the respective utilities, the quality of the television programme determines the utility of the television set, and it does so probably more than the differences in the quality of the television set itself which, being a market good, receives in modern welfare theory a preferential treatment over less countable and measurable collective goods such as television programmes.

Giving human welfare a more holistic interpretation, the activities necessary for achieving end-results such as commodities come into focus. The *process* as a whole becomes the relevant welfare determinant. We may define process as *a*, a composite of activities *b*, pursued in a period of time *c*, to generate an end-result. Out of this complex welfare entity, welfare theory has traditionally cut the slice 'end-result' elevating it to the sole determinant of human welfare. Category *b* has utility only in its 'quality of absence' as leisure time. *a* has, besides the generation of the end-result, no intrinsic welfare significance which would propose a treatment as a utility variable *sui generis*. *b* receives a peculiar twist since it is defined as the residual from total time available and the end-results (economic commodities) rendered during that time (measured usually in its opportunity cost, the wage rate). Having reduced leisure from a process (its very nature) to an end-result there is no conceivable procedure which would allow us to assess the utility of the process itself. Whether individuals develop their full potential as human beings or are bored and frustrated during their free time is, following the doctrine, irrelevant to the welfare of these individuals. A differentiation is allowed for only when end-results (cars, television sets or sports equipment) can be introduced explicitly as utility variables and constitute a 'coupled consumption' jointly with leisure time. But this procedure implies that the more durable consumer goods we consume the more psychological satisfaction we can derive from leisure time – a disturbing result, but a significant one for the delineation of a *Weltanschauung* (of which the concept is only a product) which equates material affluence with human well-being. While leisure at least in its reduced form becomes a utility variable, the analysis was further narrowed when dealing with *a* by not even considering a reduction process but simply leaving it as a utility variable. If we were to tell the man in the street that his working conditions do not affect his well-being, he would probably make the retort that economists are difficult people to understand. Tsuru's remarks (Chapter 7) are quite to the point. As long as we do not understand the true meaning of the distinction made by the Greeks between 'work' as performed by 'free citizens' and 'labour' as performed by 'slaves' a proper assessment of welfare is hard indeed.

The current mode of equating welfare with economic commodities on a theoretical level has its empirical counterpart in the G.N.P. as a welfare indicator. The recent emphasis on the limitations of the G.N.P. as a welfare indicator constitutes itself a forceful critic of modern welfare theory.[28] Various improvements have been suggested. Their aim is basically to substitute G.N.P. as an index of *production* by a 'measure of economic welfare (M.E.W.)' which is an index of *consumption*.[29] This brings to attention that production after all has an ultimate purpose which economic theory has to acknowledge, that, specifically, some of the consumption items are 'regretable' while others are 'instrumental', that many final goods are in fact rather intermediate goods, that 'actual' differs from 'sustainable' *per capita* consumption, and so on.[30] It leaves, however, unanswered the question to what extent the consumption index represents a corresponding '*state of consciousness*' – the ultimate test of welfare. It does not solve the problem of drawing a distinction between 'economic' and 'human' welfare. The two are separable for an analytical instance, but they are intrinsically combined in reality. The validity of a welfare theory crucially depends on the recognition that the gap between consumption and psychological satisfaction is greater than the gap between production and consumption (as welfare indicators) and that 'psychological satisfaction' is the relevant variable which has to be defined and measured – this has, of course, long been acknowledged by biologists and psychologists. It seems unreasonable to further ignore their results and to work with a different assumption about human well-being. Biologists and psychologists today go one step further. Not only do they measure psychological satisfaction or well-being under 'given' conditions, in the language of economics traditionally a set of consumer goods, but they try to show how it is possible for a person to stimulate 'pleasure centres' (for example own control of alpha-wave frequency in a person's E.E.G.) and thereby to increase psychological satisfaction.[31] The economist's way of increasing 'psychological satisfaction' is to provide more consumer goods. The fact, however, that psychological satisfaction can be derived from an identical commodity (including leisure) to various degrees does not prove the unmeasurability or subjective nature of psychological satisfaction but rather that it constitutes the relevant welfare indicator and the 'final' point of reference in a utility variable.

The N.N.P. and N.N.C (net national consumption) will not necessarily become superfluous as welfare indicators; the conclusions derived from their size and components with a view to human welfare will become substantiated and more representative, and eventually – to dare to look beyond the immediate 'researchable frontier' (Leibenstein) – they will be supplemented by a concept called *N.N.S.* (*net national satisfactions*) being an aggregation of final goods measured in units of *well-being* or *states of consciousness.*

The final goal of any scientific inquiry is a general theory: in welfare economics this means a *general theory of welfare.* This has been attempted by choosing axioms and by formalising the conceivable alternatives within these axioms. The axioms in fact were not 'general' in the sense which would mean validity for all historical instances. Their historical nature, however, has been veiled by the assumption that choices among axioms are based solely on value judgements. Subsequently, the degree of formalisation has been confused with the degree of generalisation.

In the future any alternative approach to the axiomatic and formalised treatment of welfare will start – following the general mode of theorising – with the facts. This means, first that various concepts in their empirical meaning have to be made operational.

The discussion on subsistence utilities indicated that in some areas of utility an empirically objectifiable ordering is conceivable and eventually can constitute part of a set of 'empirical axioms'. In the areas of supplementary utilities the ordering of utilities will certainly encounter all the 'old' well-known problems welfare theory has been tackling, but the principal acceptance of an empirical approach will also open new vistas for interdisciplinary research with biologists, psychologists and sociologists, contributing to the solution of these problems to an extent not imaginable from the position of the old antiseptic formalism. Welfare theory, in taking this first step, will have to be less ambitious than it was in the past. It is likely that various *partial theories of welfare* will have to be developed *first* which only at a later stage can be combined into a comprehensive and consistent general theory of welfare. As empirical deepening progresses it becomes obvious that categories like commodity, utility, satisfaction, or properties like divisibility, marginal adjustment, comparability, homogeneity, external effects, complementariness, or concepts like cardinal, ordinal, lexical measurability or ordering have validity only for specific realms of welfare. The search for the 'magic unit' which links all these individual phenomena, properties and concepts might not be the theoretically most promising path and might not be a feasible one at all. Units of satisfaction, a *numéraire* which makes them comparable, statements or hypotheses about the ordering will have to be developed, but they are to be rather the result of empirically founded partial theories of welfare rather than *a priori* categories (if they are not to become empirically void as the formalised marginal equivalences of existing welfare theory). A major condition for the usefulness of a 'general theory of welfare' then might be to provide criteria which allow plausible or empirically founded statements about the actual relevance and application of the 'partial theories of welfare', or respectively which state how the partial components are combined or structured in the over-all general welfare theory. The empirical determination of welfare will allow us to make statements about the historical dynamic role of specific sets of axioms such as the 'assumption axioms' of consumer sovereignty, democratic transformation from individual to social welfare, or 'conceptual axioms' such as the impossibility of interpersonal comparisons.

The formulation of two partial welfare theories, one for developed countries and one for less-developed countries, with likely quite different axioms, concepts, and hypotheses seems to be the most pressing theoretical task for the immediate future.

VII Proposition 4: The Need to View Economics as Political Economy

Political economy analyses (I) the distribution of the national produce or social dividend between social classes or other social entities (II) in the context of specific societal and material conditions applying a theory of value. Against this background of definition, *classical economics* clearly *was* political economy – in fact, the definition itself reiterates in general terms Ricardo's definition of political economy.[32] Smith, Ricardo, Malthus, Mill and Marx, all shared the view that the theoretical explanation of the 'laws' which govern the distribution of wages, profits and rents to labourers, capitalists and landlords constitutes the principal problem of political economy.

As the discussion on the current paradigm suggests, neoclassical theory does not provide a genuine explanation for the distribution among social classes (I); and, concluding from the discussion on a long-run view in economics, major long-run explanatory variables are kept constant in that theory, and consequently do not explain the objective context to which (I) applies; finally, the prevailing value theories do not provide a sufficient basis for evaluation once the neoclassical 'conditions of absence' are abandoned and the classical criteria introduced. Proposition 4 suggests a reconstruction of political economy along the lines of the classical definition: first, pertaining to (I), to integrate into economic theory distribution as an explanatory variable and as a relevant welfare entity; secondly, pertaining to (II), to assess the prevailing value theories and their supporting axioms under the present societal and material conditions.

Since both neoclassical theory and the 'new' welfare economics do not include distribution in their theoretical framework, the integration of *distribution* as an explanatory variable has to be accomplished on both (*A*) *positive analytical* and (*B*) *normative* grounds.

Without going here into the controversy between the two Cambridge Schools, it should be clear from Harrod's contribution (Chapter 4) that distribution has a considerable impact on the production in an economy. Income earners pertaining to different social classes and income groups have different ideas about what fractions of their income to save and consume. Consequently, any shift in this structure leads to a variation in the level of aggregate saving and consumption. The order of causation from distribution to production comes clearly into focus in Harrod's model because the capital–output ratio is kept constant, and any variation of the output depends on the fraction of the income saved, which in turn depends on the distribution of income. The proposition to have, ideally, the actual growth rate approach the optimal growth rate means, first, to let the actual savings rate approach the required savings rate, and, second, to let the distribution of income approach a pattern which yields the required savings rate. The causation nexus as propounded in Harrod's model had to escape the neoclassical premise which meant keeping the savings rate constant thus providing no way of explaining the variables, such as distribution, which determine the variations in the savings rate.

As a consequence of the prevailing production-function orientated approach, little empirical research has been conducted, as Myrdal recalls (Chapter 5), on the effects of the income distribution on production, savings and investment. This appears as a gross deficiency particularly when reference is made to less-developed countries since there exists a direct link between income distribution and labour productivity as is evident from the discussion on subsistence utilities. In the macro context the income distribution determines – as Leibenstein has shown elsewhere – the variables of savings, investment, *per capita* income and population, and may consequently have a dramatic impact on the determination of the equilibrium position of a system under Malthusian conditions (for example determining that proportion of the population which is to survive under given resource conditions).[33]

As for (*B*), the acceptance of an empirical treatment of welfare suggested earlier (see pp. 19–29) will open new vistas for a prolific discussion on the distribution question. First of all, there could be given more substance to the analysis of distribution, since the distribution would not be merely conceived of in terms of income but as *distribution of a comprehensive set of welfare entities*. The results would have a significant impact on the assessment of distribution policies whatever normative desideratum as distributional criterion is chosen.

An empirical welfare theory would give distributional judgements dual support by (*a*) stating the relevant *utility variables* and attaching empirical *weights* to them, and (*b*) making statements about the *levels* of utility which *individuals* or *groups* of a society can derive from a given set of welfare entities defined in (*a*). Confronted with the gross choice between subsistence and supplementary utilities, the members of most societies will give absolute priority to the former; thus the lexical-ordering principle in this realm of welfare choice arises. The assumption of this choice underlies Tsuru's proposal (Chapter 7) to start economics with the specification of a basket of 'civil minima' and is implied in Tinbergen's proposal (Chapter 2) to design models of development where mass poverty in the early phases of development is excluded. Such proposals contain the value judgement that all men are equal in their right to survive. However, the postulation of the value judgement emerges from the assessment of a specific *historical* situation, and therefore has a core of concrete *objectivity* of its own. Progress in the empirical concretisation of welfare may help to ascertain a sequence of normative propositions, say types of equity postulates or their degree of implementation in various phases of development, or provide criteria for evaluating distributional propositions as they affect social welfare in *various developmental phases* of a society.

Assuming (*a*) as given, say, the type of utility and the developmental phase, (*b*) will show the interpersonal differences in the level of utilities, or, more often expressed in terms of its reciprocal, the *structure of needs* for that welfare entity. For instance, in the realm of subsistence utilities, differences in the needs for welfare entities, such as for food and shelter, may be typically expressed by the age structure of a population, the share of the working population, or the professional structure. When dealing with supplementary utilities, more subjective features expressed in various biological differences, in the widest sense, will be relevant for the determination of a need structure.[34] The analytical description and empirical assessment of a need structure is likely to have the more welfare theoretical as well as political significance, the closer the society referred to is to the subsistence level. The deviation of a distributional scheme from a welfare theoretically assessed need structure may deprive a group of individuals of their basic needs causing malnutrition or premature death of that group. The theoretical assessment of a structure of interpersonal utility differentials does not, of course, render superfluous a distributional value judgement. But it suggests, as in (*a*), that the effects of the distributional schemes on human welfare differ with the *per capita* level of welfare entities a society can provide, and that, consequently, these differences in the impact of distribution on welfare may favour certain distributional criteria to be applied in specific development phases of a society.

A key problem of a 'new' political economy, as indicated in the chapters by Tsuru, Kapp and Myrdal, consists in describing and assessing the production, consumption and distribution relationships within the context of *changing objective conditions* (kept constant in contemporary economics). Both value theories, the *market price theory of value* and the *labour theory of value* do not bring forth a system of exchange ratios or of relative prices which would determine the production, consumption and distribution relationships in a way that a social-welfare function desirable in the light of a conceivable 'good' society can be satisfied. From the point of view of a holistic welfare assessment, both value theories are inoperational since they exclude welfare entities other than economic commodities. A new valuation procedure reflecting the relative values of the entire set of utility variables according to a holistic interpretation of welfare is required. Both value theories fail similarly to provide an objective basis for assessing the value of the production factors under the prevailing long-run conditions. There is no criteria implied in the market price which would assess the present use of non-renewable resources as a function of the total finite stock available; nor does it allow us to assess the consumption or production behaviour with a view to the equilibrium conditions of the ecological system, the health of the working population, or the ultimate end of technical progress. The labour theory of value fails even more as a rational device for the valuation of the production costs since it treats only direct and indirect (= capital) labour as a value-creating factor, excluding natural resources as a genuine source of value. (This has led for instance to the deterioration of the environment in Eastern European countries comparable to that of Western countries.) Finally, both value theories become increasingly inoperational as bases for social distribution. Besides the indicated failure to provide an objective assessment of the production costs, a highly technology-intensive production process makes it increasingly impossible to determine the shares of factors, either in terms of direct or indirect labour, or as marginal contributions to the social product, and consequently makes it near impossible to derive a reliable distributional judgement.

Scientific procedures of *evaluation* will play a crucial role in a new political economy. The evaluation process may have an *objective* basis provided by *science.* Biology and medicine will be crucial in giving substance to the social-welfare function, and the findings of geology and technological forecasting will have an impact on the evaluation of non-renewable resources.[35] However, the values held by different people, social classes and groups about various social issues call for the delineation of procedures which allow a genuine evaluation in a normative or political sense.[36] For example, people may have consumption preferences, *X*, which threatens the values of environmental conservation, *Y*. The implementation of value *Y* may interfere with the axiomatic value of consumer sovereignty, *Z*. A theory with predictive power as well as any conceivable 'optimum regime' will depend on the assessment of the variables *X*, *Y*, *Z*, and not on a procedure which relies merely on the assessment of one or two of the variables. In contemporary market theory, for instance, the value *Y* does not appear as an explanatory variable, the value *Z* is assumed to be 'good' and kept axiomatically constant, and the value *X* is the outcome of undisputed rational consumer behaviour. In the light of the changes to be expected, any future theory with predictive or normative significance must include the evaluation of the members of a society (including the economists!) in terms of a *comprehensive set of values* which goes far beyond the traditional concept of market preferences.[37]

The implementation of a social-welfare function of the holistic type encompassing utility variables such as environmental and process variables, distribution according to a rational social consensus, and the implementation of appropriate institutions and behavioural premises cannot be achieved by the market. The *state* as the relevant decision-making unit and 'optimiser' is called for. As long as the optimisation process can rely on the institutions of the market and market behaviour, the neglect of the state, as evident in neoclassical theory, cannot jeopardise the quality of this optimum. If the major phenomena which demand evaluation (such as a holistic welfare function or institutional changes) lie not within the market context but in the realm of government competence then the neglect of the state may well signify the irrelevance of such theory.

Once the role of the state as the major decision-maker is probable and accepted, a framework for rational government action is required. Thus, the quest for *government planning* is spelled out by Tinbergen (Chapter 2), but is also referred to (though for different reasons) by Harrod, Kapp and Tsuru in their essays. The earlier suggested empirical specification of the social-welfare function and the application of a time horizon which reaches beyond that of market decisions proves not only relevant for a positive analytical theory with predictive quality but constitutes also a necessary condition for social planning if it is to be consistent over a time span relevant for major decisions affecting society.

The endogenisation of variables of the body politic into economic models, as has been attempted by the new school of *politometrics*, is instrumental for conclusive statements about the probability of the actual implementation of plans, government policies or social objectives.[38] As far as the economic and political systems in these models are kept constant,[39] an extension of the (simulation and empiricist) models will prove necessary when the social desiderata demand changes in these systems themselves, for example changes in institutions and behavioural premises of the two systems.

VIII Concluding Remarks

We may conclude with some reflections on the earlier question of whether a paradigm shift will occur in the future development of economics. If economics develops along the lines suggested in the four propositions, such development will constitute a paradigm shift. Even if one gives the current paradigm a wider meaning than that defined in terms of neoclassical theory, allowing for various 'syntheses' and extensions, the propositions suggested – a holistic perspective, an interdisciplinary system approach, analytical emphasis on long-run variables, the focus on empirical relevance, and the acceptance of economics as political economy – may induce changes in the basic structure of the science of economics which might be called a paradigm shift. Whether such a paradigm shift will occur in the foreseeable future will depend on the possibility of stretching the current paradigm of neoclassical theory and of paying the costs of the failures which result when it is applied to solve current problems. Either of these has its limitations. The tensions and costs are likely to multiply at an exponential rate. And with it grows the evidence that novel approaches are needed. In a way, we are reminded of the ferry-boat captain who tells his passengers that he knows every rock in the harbour. When he crashes into one, exclaims, 'for example, this one!' In the learned words of

Whitehead, 'It takes an uncommon kind of mind to see the significance of the obvious.' It is the purpose of this book to make the evidence explicit and to indicate the directions in which appropriate approaches will and should emerge.

Part Two

Selected Topics

2 More Empirical Research

Jan Tinbergen

I Introduction

While I consider very useful any attempt to answer the question of what the future development of the science of economics will be, I expect rather divergent answers from those invited to formulate an answer. Almost as a matter of course every worker in some fields of our discipline will consider his speciality the most important – for this is the reason why he works on it. His choice will partly be based on what problems the present world is faced with and so illustrates Gunnar Myrdal's old statement on the forces at work in such choices.[1] But there remain subjective preferences of a more random nature which co-determine our personal curiosity and there remain the environments from which each of us has originated; environments which differ. And there are elements of the technique of scientific work which fit one student better than another. Thus, for example, I am not going to touch monetary problems, since I feel less fit to deal with them; this does not imply that, in my opinion, monetary problems are not important: on the contrary. Yet, I am going to take up some problems emotionally closer to my personal approach.

II Future Problems Demanding Solution by Economists

My essay in this book will be arranged around three problem areas which I feel are important and which fit my approach.

Throughout I will refer to them under the headings *A*, *B* and *C* to be explained in this section.

A. *Problems of income distribution* and more precisely the problem whether a development process with less mass misery in the beginning can be designed constitute the first problem area. So far we have almost uniformly observed development processes where, in the take-off phase, mass consumption was low and deteriorating. Britain showed this picture in the early nineteenth century; the Soviet Union showed it during the 1930s and India (like many other poor countries of today) according to Dandekar and Rath shows a reduction in consumption *per capita* of the lowest urban decile during the 1960s.[2] It would be important to design socio-economic policies (national or international) of development not characterised by this feature of mass suffering. This requires at least knowledge about how income distribution is determined and by what means of deliberate policy it can be changed while not impairing the forces making for development.

B. Another set of problems can be grouped around the question of which *division of labour between poor and rich countries* makes an optimal contribution to the development of low-income countries. Several questions of practical policy can be handled adequately only if we know what industries (in the widest sense) should be developed in both types of countries and what instruments of economic policy can be applied in order to attain such goals. What role can or should be played by trade policies, investment planning, subsidisation of industries and probably other means of guidance to development?

C. A third set of problems has arisen quite recently around the intensification of *air and water pollution as well as the exhaustion of natural resources*. The contract research undertaken by Professors Forrester[3] and Meadows[4] at the Massachusetts Institute of Technology at the request of the 'Club of Rome' constitutes one approach to this problem area, and another approach has been chosen by Professor Leontief of Harvard University.[5] So far the approaches have been given in the form of attempts at forecasting future developments and the results point to many possibilities of disaster. Everybody, including the authors mentioned, agree that only first steps have been made. What next steps are necessary, what data do we need and what policies can be devised to minimise the extent of possible disasters?

III What Theoretical Frameworks will be Adequate for the Solution of these Problems?

A. This problem area requires, as a minimum, the integration of two sub-areas, to be indicated as *development theory* and the *theory of income distribution.* In both fields numerous approaches have already been attempted and the beginning of an understanding of some crucial issues has been made. For the ultimate application of these or other theories we will have to concentrate on the planning aspect rather than on the analytical or explanatory aspect as I tried to set out elsewhere.[6] This will automatically imply that theories have to be developed which can be applied practically and keep us away from theorising at too far a distance from observable and measurable phenomena (cf. also pp. 44–5). This is a useful requirement because we are aware now of the necessity of an interdisciplinary approach. More particularly, a number of social, cultural and political variables will have to be included, and measurement is less advanced in these fields of scientific research than in economics. While the production process remains one of the central phenomena of development (and hence economic theories of production are bound to have their place in any theory of development), human attitudes in the co-operation of production factors, with their social and cultural bounds must supplement the purely economic theory of production. Bad health, lack of communication between castes, lack of education or the type of education prevailing will influence the productivity of human beings. The cultural and political institutions in which social life is organised will co-determine the outcome of a production process and, perhaps even more, of the processes of distribution and consumption. The aims set and the aims neglected by a country's government will limit some possibilities of increasing the welfare of the population, which will be considered the more essential criterion of appraisal of development by the majority of a country's population. Alongside technical laws of production, therefore, the country's institutions determine the outcome of production and consumption, and consumption will have its feedback on productivity. Planning for development must make an attempt to take into account, in whatever simplified way imposed by the information available, these various interactions. I think it is no scientific imperialism to state that, so far, the best general framework to be used has been the framework of economic planning; but the contents within this framework must be considerably richer than what used to be the one-sided economic contents as seen by Westerners.

With regard to *income distribution* the present situation of the theoretical framework is probably less developed even than for the process of development. The various theories of income distribution now available have less in common than the theories of development. First, they range from almost completely stochastic theories (that is theories based on random forces) to almost completely deterministic theories. We hardly know how large the element of chance in income distribution is. Secondly, even the relatively elementary economic concepts of demand for and supply of various skill combinations have been used only recently by a few authors.[7] Other authors only consider supply elements without discussing demand except in an indirect way by the introduction of unemployment.[8] The relative importance of economic forces as compared with traditional and institutional ones is a subject of considerable controversy, for instance between economists and sociologists. Within the economic discussion of income-distribution theory the relative importance of wealth and skill as two competing explanatory factors is a matter for debate. When it comes to the planning of income distribution, the influence that may be exerted by some different means, such as taxes, low-cost social services and education, is not too well-known. More generally, the question whether experiences of industrialised countries can be used for the design of an incomes policy for a poor country weighs heavily. Moreover, some basic controversies about what income distribution should be aimed at still exist in developed countries. Some economists take a view of complete agnosticism, referring the question to moralists or ethics, while others, among them S.-C. Kolm, are prepared to formulate some criteria in the shape of economic criteria, admitting that some ethical postulates have been added.[9] In the same way it is possible to make progress in the measurement of utility or welfare functions enabling us to give more exact shape to the aims of income distribution. Apart from some ethical principles, some methodological premises have to be accepted, however, and most economists do not like to call this 'economics'. Among the principles one has to adhere to in order to arrive at more exact formulations two stand out, one ethical, and one methodological. The ethical principle is that it is assumed that all men are equal except for the parameters which can be measured and which show inequality. One might refer to this principle as the principle of the 'fundamental equality' of men. The methodological principle may be that, among the alternative theories which are able to explain observed attitudes, the simplest is used as long as it is not contradicted by new observations. This principle has long been applied in physics and is not without success in the field of practical applications.

B. For decades a number of alternative theories of *international trade* have been adhered to by economists. We will briefly remind the reader of some of them. Before doing so we should again emphasise that, for political application, only part of the set of theories can be used, depending on the measurability of the main concepts used and on the presence of 'action parameters' or 'instruments of economic policy'. Moreover, a distinction should be made between positive and normative theories.

In a recent survey G. C. Hufbauer[10] mentions the Heckscher–Ohlin theory, long considered the best theory, normative as well as, under conditions of no impediments to trade, the long-run positive theory. Formulated as briefly as possible, it says that each country should (or will) have the industries (in its most general sense) requiring the same factor mix as the country is endowed with. Looked at as a (comparative-static) long-term theory it does not preclude changes over time in any of the variables considered. In that restricted sense it can be considered dynamic. The author mentions six alternative approaches, to be called the (1) human-capital, (2) economies-of-scale, (3) stage-of-production, (4) technological-gap, (5) product-cycle and (6) simularity-of-preferences approaches. (I am indebted to P. Terhal for this summary.) The only real alternative to the Heckscher–Ohlin theory seems to me to be (3) the stage of production theory, where it is suggested that each country starts with specialisation in consumer goods' exports and gradually 'climbs up' to the preceding stages: semi-manufactured goods, processed raw materials, capital goods. Industrialisation is considered identical with import substitution here, but this clearly limits the scope of the theory, especially for small countries, but more generally for countries whose comparative advantage lies in the processing of raw materials. It may be part of a positive theory for a situation with considerable trade impediments, but it cannot be accepted as a normative theory. Theories using (1) human-capital, (2) economies-of-scale and (4) technological-gap approaches can, in principle, be integrated into the Heckscher–Ohlin system. The product-cycle theory (5) looks interesting and might be integrated also, but their concrete elaboration requires huge quantities of data, probably increasing in the order in which the theories have been mentioned. The similarity-of-preferences theory (6) deals with a demand aspect; what matters seems to be simply the composition of world demand rather than whether preferences differ.

C. The framework of *theories* to be used as the basis for *policies against the destruction of the environment* again will have to be interdisciplinary to a high extent. Clearly, most of the restrictions human society is subject to are of a biological, chemical or physical nature. One way of illustrating this is the approach chosen by Professor Leontief. While the coefficients of his input–output theory of the past can be said to be technological coefficients, this is true also for the extensions Leontief has given to his own theory by the introduction of the coefficients describing the emissions, by various man-made production processes, of polluting by-products such as sulphur dioxide, nitrogen oxides, and so on. One can imagine an even further extension of the input–output theory, extending it also to natural processes such as the regeneration of air and water by elements of the natural environment and further extending it in order also to include the consumption or the production of what formerly were called free goods.

There will also be a need, however, to extend the theory of economic policy. Depending on the results of the natural limitations we may need a set of new policy parameters, such as taxes on some type of pollution or polluting activities, mentioned by Mishan,[11] rationing or even prohibiting some production processes. Another possible policy instrument is the use of subsidies for specific types of research for clean processes. Another possibility is the implementing of instruments to attain a less unequal income distribution, which brings us back to a subject mentioned under *A*. For the purposes of reducing inequality in incomes, whether in developing countries or in countries facing pollution or the exhaustion of resources, one central issue is whether this can be done without reducing too much the incentives to work or to learn. In both cases the whole political order may be at stake and methods must be developed to compare various social orders, as suggested by Kornai,[12] and to find criteria of appraisal of different social orders as recommended by Van den Doel.[13]

IV Which Methods of Research in Economics and Related Fields are likely to undergo the most Radical Changes?

I feel rather strongly that the emphasis, within economic science, should be more on empirical rather than on theoretical research.

I want to add two further specifications however. With the development of econometrics it seemed as if the shift towards more empirical research had started. But within econometrics there appeared a further tendency to concentrate too strongly on methods of verification or testing of assumptions and too weakly on the collection of well-devised new statistical material.

On the other side of the discipline of economic research relatively too much attention is given to the collection and interpretation of short-term – month-to-month or even day-to-day – movements mostly serving speculative activities of either speculators, or traders, or the combined activity of production and speculation.

The empirical studies I am advocating should be directed at more fundamental knowledge about the operation of economies (or even societies) and the basic concepts of our science. Some examples of the operation have already been mentioned before. As an example of a fundamental concept to which too little empirical work has been devoted we may take the concept of utility or welfare.

Although relatively neglected there is a nevertheless already voluminous stock of empirical studies, due to diversified activities over the last fifty years. This stock may be subdivided into three parts. First, we have some knowledge of individual ratios or coefficients useful for planning purposes. I think of production functions, including capital–output and employment–output ratios, or rates of growth of some types of activity. I also think of empirical studies such as by Balassa on effective protection[14] and many more examples could be quoted. The second part of our stock of empirical knowledge consists of single relations or equations such as Engel curves, demand functions and price (or supply) equations; there are also some useful balance equations.

The third part consists of consistent sets of relations, or models. Here we have Keynesian macro models and a number of refinements of them, some of which lead to complicated econometric models.[15] We also have models of activity analysis, including input–output models and their recent refinements. We have models, for instance one constructed by Cohen which combines economic and extra-economic (so-called social) variables[16] and we have them not only for single countries, but for large parts of the world.[17] Each of them can be used either for purposes of analysis and forecasts or for the use of planners.

It seems appropriate here to point to two different methods of deriving or constructing models, discussed intensively about a decade ago, namely (1) models reflecting the results of testing existing theories and (2) empiricist models. The distinction is not quite as sharp as the phrases suggest. Models of the first kind may not necessarily reflect the original theory their authors had in mind when starting on construction. In the process they may have been forced to change the theory so as to fit the observations better.

While, nevertheless, such models may be said to have a socio-economic theory behind them, this is not so in an empiricist model. Here the authors claim that they are unbiassed by theory and that the facts only have 'spoken'. This was the attitude with Mitchell's business cycle research so well described by Burns.[18] With increasing understanding of the nature of the business cycle the method was abandoned and almost forgotten. Recently, however, the need for this first phase of 'reconnaissance' in a new field, has gained respect again, and several methods of statistical research, designed for the purpose, have been applied or developed. Factor analysis was one of the oldest, first applied in educational research; discriminant analysis is another example and both have been used extensively in the field of development theory, especially by Mrs Adelman and Mrs Morris.[19] I must admit, however, that my admiration for the daring methods used by these colleagues does not prevent me from considering their schemas as starting points only for theory-based models, which need new testing after the theoretical background has been found. Of course this desire may reflect an overly deterministic attitude on my side.

One feature of the work by Mrs Adelman and her (various) associates is their push for measurement of phenomena previously thought to be non-measurable. I fully share their opinion that progress in our understanding can only be based on this push and this implies that large numbers of phenomena discussed verbally by fellow economists will have to be measured. As I set out elsewhere,[20] even physics does not measure its variables in a completely objective way, but by a 'majority vote', and in my opinion the majority required for a statement to become objective is less than 100 per cent, especially in the social sciences.

After this general discussion of desirable changes in emphasis towards the more empirical approaches let us discuss some concrete examples within each of the three problem areas we have chosen.

A. *Income distribution* is not merely an economic phenomenon, but has to be seen in a wider sociological context. Even so we may first discuss some approaches by economists. Considerable attention has been given, mainly by American economists, to the relationship between schooling, represented by the number of years of school attendance, and income. The concept of human capital has been developed, which we shall encounter also when dealing with problem area *B*, that is the international division of labour. Economists such as T. W. Schultz,[21] G. Becker[22] and others have attempted to estimate the yield of investment in education and compared it with yield of investment in the traditional sense, that is in capital goods. In a number of cases they have found that the former surpasses the latter. Subsequently, J. Mincer,[23] T. W. Schultz[24] and B. R. Chiswick[25] have suggested the theory that income differences are largely due to differences in schooling. The latter are explained by the individual decisions on the number of years of schooling and it seems intuitively obvious that among the determinants of these decisions the expected yields play their part. Since several tests of this simple economic theory of income distribution were not completely satisfactory, and the operation of other forces could be expected to interfere, the theory was extended in various directions. Let us first discuss some economic extensions.

In an early stage Chiswick added as a determinant the rate of growth of average income of the community studied.[26] He found a considerable influence of this variable: quick development having a positive influence on income inequality as measured by the fifth percentile from the top, divided by median income. Similarly, he found a strong influence when using the lowest quartile of income, divided by median income.

Later on, the need to introduce, in a more general and also more concrete way, demand factors has been put forward by the same authors and by myself simultaneously.[27] Whereas my American colleagues used employment percentage as a demand indicator, I proposed to use the demand structure as shown by the large sectors (agriculture, manufacturing, trade and transportation, and other services), combined with the relative size of these sectors in each geographical unit studied.

Without any doubt non-economic factors play their part as well. For some time already it was customary to take into account the social strata at the income receivers' start. A penetrating analysis has been presented by L. Soltow[28] and another one by T. Husén.[29] In theory other variables describing innate features are also acting and empirical work is in process with Schmölders[30] and Brinkmann.[31] A huge mass of hardly used material is available

TABLE 1

*Most relevant variables found by Mrs Adelman in an analysis of various income shares in developing countries**

Income share of	*Explanatory variables in order of relevance*
60 per cent poorest	1. Dualism; 2. Develop. potential and G.N.P.; 3. Education.
20 per cent poorest	1. Dualism; 2. Agr. productivity; 3. Agr. organisation; 4. Social mobility.
Middle-income groups	1. Size of middle class; 2. Natural resources; 3. Education and participation.
Wealthiest 20 per cent	1. Dualism; 2. Govt econ. activity; 3. Education and natural resources.
Wealthiest 5 per cent	1. Natural resources; 2. Education and govt econ. Activity; 3. Cult. and ethn. homogeneity; 4. Govt econ. activity.

* The word 'education' has been used here instead of Mrs Adelman's 'human resources'.

in job evaluation and the corresponding tests on persons applying for a job or being considered in career planning. Recently Mrs Adelman applied ingenious statistical techniques on income distribution data for about forty developing countries and found the variables listed in Table 1 to be the most relevant (in order of relevance).[32]

Future research may be conceived along various lines. First, some of the non-economic explanatory variables suggested by Mrs Adelman's reconnaissance may be integrated into socio-economic models of the theory-based type, implying that these variables themselves will then be variables of the model and will find their explanation in other equations of such a model. The models so obtained may then be used for planning purposes, which implies that some variables are considered means or instruments of socio-economic policies. Among other things the problem mentioned earlier (p. 40) may then be analysed: is it possible to have development without deterioration of the standard of living of the masses right from the beginning of the development process? No doubt other problems will be encountered in the attempts to solve the focal problem. Among these the problem will arise to what extent incentives not yet used can be introduced into the set of means of socio-economic policies. Research could be extended on the impact of incentives on human behaviour, furthering work done already by Fields and Stanbury.[33]

B. Some of the theories on *international trade*, positive as well as normative, have already been discussed earlier (see pp. 43–4).

Correspondingly some recent research on international trade and some recommendations for future research will be now discussed.

A fair amount of positive research has been undertaken in the last few decades, research that is to describe and analyse the existing structure of international trade. Here, advantage could be taken of the existing trade statistics, which show a subdivision into thousands of single items, far more than the best production statistics. Even so, some of the studies have been based on production statistics. Significant contributions have been made by Chenery and a number of collaborators[34] which show the presence of some common features in the patterns of production of a large number of countries at all levels of development. Predominant industries in the earliest phase (income *per capita*, \$100; population, 10 million) are food, beverages and textiles, whereas at a later stage (income *per capita*, \$600; same population) capital goods become relatively more important. The size of the country is represented by its G.N.P. as well as by its population and both variables influence a country's structure. As a matter of course also the natural endowments of the country concerned play their part, especially for small countries where the primary endowment may be very one-sided.

Linnemann[35] has shown the influence on trade as a whole exerted by the size of the trade partners, represented by total incomes as well as total population, their distance (representing both transportation and communication costs, the latter also reflecting cultural differences) and their membership of such groupings as the British Commonwealth, the French zone, and so on. The mobility of a large number of tradable commodities has been studied by Herman,[36] who shows that most industrial and agricultural products are traded the world round, the exception being a group of 'heavy' materials, usually at a low level of processing.

Lary[37] found a clear relationship between import impediments and labour-intensity of the products produced in the United States.

Among recent research of a normative character Herman's attempt[38] to find the optimum capital-intensity of the industries to be developed by a given country is an example of how such problems should be tackled with the aid of empirical material. A first attempt to present a sketch of the optimum division of labour among countries has been made,[39] so far without provoking improved alternatives in figures. Various refinements and corrections are in the process of being applied. One of them attempts to apply a finer subdivision of human capital or skills than had been used in the study just quoted. Another brings the main idea of the semi-input–output method into the picture. This means that a number of immobile industries (industries producing non-tradables) are added and that their necessary output and employment for the expansion of each mobile industry are calculated, that is the 'bunch of activities' which are inseparable, because of the phenomenon of non-tradeability of a number of inputs to each mobile industry, are taken as the true units of expansion. As a rule, the dispersion in capital intensity is less between bunches than between the industries producing tradeables. In addition, employment of the same order of magnitude is provided by the immobile and the mobile part of a bunch. Included automatically in the pieces of research mentioned is the answer to the question whether or not some primary products should be processed in the country of origin. Generally this is questionable when the processing requires huge capitals, but a more precise case-by-case study using actual transportation costs must be recommended.

Finally, after this very brief description of research already published or started, some fields for further refinement may be suggested. More reliable answers to the question which industries should be developed in each country can be obtained if a much finer subdivision of production statistics were available. Refinement of our knowledge regarding capital-intensity should be aimed at in two directions. A 'horizontal' refinement, meaning the distinction of more products, and a 'vertical' refinement, meaning the distinction of more successive steps in each production process, would be very helpful. Moreover, services are often not part of the activities covered by production statistics and here too statistical data giving considerable detail are desirable.

Recently a new question has been added to the main question and the answers given so far: to what extent will our answers have to be revised in the light of pollution and other environmental problems? It is conceivable, as has been suggested, to let the developing countries develop some of the polluting industries (chemicals, oil refining) as long as the level of already existing pollution is low in many of these countries. It may raise their incomes, without, for quite some time, causing damage to them. Often, developing countries have wanted to have such industries and in fact some have them already. Pollution in developed countries may be a reason to prescribe anti-polluting installations, which raises production costs and hence makes developing countries more competitive, as long as they do not impose such equipment. For a period of ten or twenty years developing countries may profit from this competitive advantage.

C. The problems of *pollution*, just mentioned, and of the *exhaustion of natural resources* have suddenly received much more attention than before, as has been observed already (see p. 40). Subsequently we briefly indicated the new theoretical frameworks which may have to be used for their solution. It is in these fields that the need for more empirical research is especially urgent; first, in the fields of biology, chemistry and technology, but soon also in the social sciences. Once we are better informed about the restrictions of a technical, chemical or similar character, numerous questions of a social and economic nature will arise. While the necessary reductions in some activities endangering the environment may partly be attained through traditional market forces, other forces may well have to be put in action. The rate of growth of world population will, in all probability, have to be restricted, if not even reversed into a reduction of total population. In the last few years some more experience has been obtained on the impact of various conceivable measures.[40] Mass information and education may be needed and its impact studied. In a number of sectors rationing will be needed – of which some quantitative work is already available[41] – but the need for international rationing and the instruments to let it work may come up and here our experience is much more limited. Research programmes in the fields of the natural sciences and the corresponding technologies may have to be redirected and this redirection may be partly attained through socio-economic policies. Since the possibility cannot be denied that mankind is going to live under circumstances similar to what was traditionally known as a war economy and since a war economy is traditionally much more centralised than a peace-time economy, the most dramatic change that might occur a few years from now is a new concentration of economic thinking inspired by the planning approach, already defended on other grounds earlier (see p. 41).

V The Future Role of the Economist

From the examples dealt with in this essay it may be seen that there are a number of tasks for economists, several of which are of considerable importance. Whether they will be successful in performing these tasks depends, first of all, on the degree of success they will be able to attain in their own narrow fields. I already expressed my view that this success – or a lack of it – will depend to no small part on the willingness of economists to concentrate on relevant problems using a quantitative approach. It goes without saying that inventiveness in these realms will add, as a matter of course, also to their success. An important further condition for more success will lie in the ability to co-operate with representatives from other fields of activity. These would include not only scientists, but also politicians and people actually working in the production processes. For some time to come economists are in a relatively advantageous position of having manifold contacts and being near the centre of several of these activities. I think of the increased role of consultation or of the increasing numbers of economists who, in recent decades, have found their way into business and government positions. Whether they will or will not strengthen this position will depend on the attitude of co-operation, of giving operational shape to their knowledge and research, and of expressing themselves in understandable language, understandable, that is, to those with whom they have to co-operate *and* to the general public. In a well-known phrase they should enhance their credibility.

3 Micro–Micro Theory, Agent–Agent Trade and *X*-Efficiency

Harvey Leibenstein

I Control, Understanding and the Researchable Frontier

It is impossible in advance to determine the future course of economic analysis; however, some trends seem fairly clear. Governments are likely to play an increasing role in economic activities – even in primarily private-enterprise (or mixed) economies. The current difficulties that governments have in trying to manage inflation is probably in part due to a lack of understanding of some fundamental economic processes. For what it is worth, in my view, the inadequacies of current macro theories and macro models cannot be overcome entirely by more research on a macro basis. There is a sense in which all basic processes have to be reduced to an understanding of individual reactions, or the reactions of micro units to the environment in which they operate. This suggests the possibility that an eventual increase in understanding even of macro phenomena may come about as a result of improvements in *micro*economic knowledge. In any event, this view forms a jumping-off point for the ideas to be sketched in this chapter.

Developments in economics are, in part, a reaction to demand – demand by governments or other organs of society for knowledge on ways of solving what are believed to be pressing economic problems. But this type of demand is hardly sufficient to create a supply of satisfactory intellectual solutions. At best all that demand can do is to provide the means to support the intellectual effort.

Some problems can only be solved in a sequence of interdependent stages some of which are prerequisites to others. In principle, we can have genuinely premature attempts to solve some types of problems. Thus it would be extremely risky to predict future developments even if we could foretell the demand for certain types of knowledge.

Another way of putting the matter is that solutions may *not* come forth simply because the problem is not *on* or *within* the 'researchable frontier'. The idea of a researchable frontier is helpful if we are to make reasonable guesses as to where a given science is going. The interconnections between different bits of knowledge may be such that we cannot solve *B* before we solve *A* and we cannot solve *C* before we solve *B*. The answer to *C* may appear to be the answer to the most pressing problem, but if *A* and *B* have not been solved then *C* may readily be beyond the researchable frontier.

In some fields the researchable frontier is fairly well established. This is not the case in economics. Hence we cannot use a knowledge of the researchable frontier as a guide to suggest where we are going as a discipline.

A basic difficulty with economics is that we do not know exactly where we are in the field. Using a medical analogy we do not know what ills we can cure and which we cannot. We do not have a clear sense of the problem areas where solutions are based on sound information and where the converse is the case. At its 'highest' levels economic writings demonstrate a high level of logical rigour, but that is really no substitute for soundly based behavioural knowledge. It would be extremely useful if, as a profession, we had considerable consensus about the applied areas within which our knowledge is effective and those where we are quite useless. The scientific status of the profession would be very different if we could tell politicians that in problem area *A* our advice is well founded and likely to be very useful but that in area *B* we really do not know very much. Or that policy *A* would lead to disastrous results but that on policy *B* we cannot have any scientific opinion. Of course, individual economists do have opinions on what we know and what we do not know. However, as a profession we do not have a consensus on these matters. One reason for this is that a considerable amount of applied economics is macroeconomic – it is highly aggregative in character. But the micro foundations of macro models have not been successfully worked out. Whether it is premature for such an achievement or not is too early to tell. Clearly these are matters that the future will have to solve. The point of these ruminations is not to paint a gloomy picture but rather to suggest reasons for my belief that (*a*) what we need is greater and deeper understanding of fundamental economic behaviour, and (*b*) we should be open-minded towards new approaches especially on the microeconomic level.

Microeconomic theory, more or less in its present form, at least on a rudimentary basis, has been around for over a century. There has been a steady deepening of our understanding of this theory but relatively little reformulation based on different postulates. I want to suggest that this is an area that is probably within the researchable frontier. In other words, we are in a position to develop models based on some deviations from the conventional postulates. The work discussed in this chapter is primarily of this nature.

Of course, I cannot really *prove* that the work proposed is within the researchable frontier in a definitive sense – that is that something of scientific value and use *will* emerge. However, I hope that this chapter will at least warrant the conclusion that this is a possibility.

In the pages that follow I plan to sketch some aspects of my recent research interests. My main aim is to suggest, even argue to some degree, that a fruitful area in which to put one's energies, in order to deepen our understanding of the behaviour of economies, is in an area that might be called 'micro–micro' theory. Of course, this suggests that conventional micro theory is not micro enough. We shall see that this approach may involve some significant departures which are in the direction towards greater realism of the fundamental behavioural assumptions.

II The Great Gap – Non-Market Economic Behaviour

Neoclassical theory is formulated 'as if' all *economic* behaviour is market behaviour and all economic decisions are directly or indirectly market decisions. In fact, micro theory is not about behaviour at all; it is about decisions. The implicit assumption underlying the theory is that what people decide, they do. Thus, if a certain exchange is decided upon it is presumed that it in fact takes place. But there are problems – *who* in a firm makes a decision when the theory tells us that a firm makes a certain type of price or quantity decision?, and *who* in the household makes the decision when the household is presumed to make a certain type of buying decision, or allocation of income decision?, and again when we talk about the utility to the buyer of something or other, whose utility exactly are we considering? If the deciders are not clearly identified how do we know whose behaviour it is that is determined? And words like 'firm' or 'household' do not clearly identify the decision-makers.

It is perhaps self-evident, although standard textbooks give a very different impression, that economic behaviour takes place in both market and non-market contexts. Two points need be emphasised: (1) only individuals make decisions, and (2) individuals behave simultaneously in market and non-market contexts. The first point cannot be overstated although once mentioned it will appear to many as self-evident. In my view, it is important to determine whether the premise that (1) organisations as such are decision-makers or, alternatively, (2) that only individuals (within and on the behalf of organisations) are decision-makers, leads to significantly different behavioural results. The second possibility raises an important question which the first appears to ignore. If it is individuals who make decisions then the organisational 'structure' (or other characteristics) are likely to make a difference. The influences that impinge on an individual are not only those external to the organisation, but also (and especially) those internal to it. Hence the significant question raised is not only how each individual in an organisation makes the decisions he faces, but how the *nature* of the organisation creates or contributes to the communication and incentive structure which influences decisions, as well as the activities that result from them.

Suppose, for ease in developing the argument, that firms in their dealings with other firms make only market decisions, that is the decisions which involve the buying and selling of outputs and inputs. But firms are a composition of many people. Does every individual in such a firm also find himself in the position where he is involved only in market decisions? There are two possible approaches. One is to presume that every individual acts in such a way so that his behaviour is consistent with the market decisions made by the firm. It is as though the firm is a market decision-making machine and every individual is a part of the machine that plays its appropriate role in the machine's mechanical behaviour. Individuals who do not play such appropriate roles are simply replaced by others that do. This is a kind of mechanistic clockwork vision of the firm. Every part contributes so that the hands of the clock show the right time. However, anyone who has worked in firms knows that this is not even the crudest approximation of what is frequently found to be the case. There are limits to individuals' capacities to co-ordinate the activities of others. Furthermore, every individual has a will of his own. Hence it seems of interest to turn the question on its head, as it were. Individuals are members of organisations. Within the organisation there is room for a great deal of non-market behaviour. There is no reason why the internals of an organisation should operate like a market. In fact, the internals of firms do not operate that way. Hence, it seems of interest to start with individuals who make choices, some of which are on a non-market basis, and then to aggregate the results of individual behaviour into group behaviour. Then we should go on to aggregate groups in order to obtain organisational (that is firm) behaviour. The very least that can be said for this approach is that it starts with the appropriate biological micro units – individual human beings. Of course, these micro units interact with each other so that we do obtain the 'molecular' behaviour of the firm. (There is a sense in which conventional micro theory may be termed 'molecular' in that it does not start with basic 'atomic' units – the individuals.) In pursuing this approach we need not ignore how the externals, that is the market behaviour, influences the internals, that is the non-market aspects. But in doing so, it is important to examine whether in fact we obtain the same results as the one we would get under the mechanistic clockwork model.

III Principal–Agent Problems

One means of seeing the importance of non-market economic behaviour is through what might be called the 'principal–agent' problem.

One of the implicit assumptions of micro theory is that all trade is carried out by principals, or by agents who behave as their principals would. It is one of the lacunae of economics that almost no analysis exists of what happens if agents and principals do not share common interests. A basic result of microeconomics is that both parties gain from any exchange. This is certainly consistent with the logic of the theory where both parties are principals, that is where people exchange on their own behalf and in their own interest. But economic life is filled with agents who spend a good deal of their time acting on the behalf of others. This is true of almost all members of firms, other than minute family firms, throughout most economies. The exception might be an agricultural sector made up entirely of farmers working their own land.

What happens when agents enter the picture? There are three trading possibilities: (1) principal–principal trade, (2) principal–agent trade, and (3) agent-agent trade. There is, of course, nothing to investigate if agents are so well instructed and so well motivated that they always engage in the type of trade that the principal would himself carry out. But, of course, neither of these assumptions need hold. Agents are not optimally instructed nor do they always see their interests as identical with that of the principals.

Suppose agents are indifferent to their principals' interests. In that case it is possible for some of the exchanges that take place between principals and other people's agents to be one-sided. The principal gains by the trade but the agent engages in some trades that reduces the utility of his principal. The net result of such trades may be a reduction in over-all efficiency. The most interesting cases, and probably most important from the view-point of the economy, are those in which agents make exchanges with other agents on behalf of their principals. Here there exists the possibility that both principals may be made worse off by some of the exchanges that take place. Such events are obviously inefficient and reduce the efficiency of the economy as a whole.

The question that leaps to mind is why should agents behave in such a manner? I would urge that we simultaneously keep in mind the obverse question, why shouldn't they? One possible answer to the first question is ignorance. There is no reason why agents should have a clear-cut conception of the utility function of their principals. This is especially true if the principals happen to be a group of individuals rather than a single individual. Secondly, the interests of agents are not the same as the interests of their principals. Thus, agents may carry out exchanges which are in their own interest but contrary to the interests of their principals. A third, and probably especially important reason, is simply slothfulness, carelessness, and so forth. Agents, in interpreting their roles, need not possess any special compelling drive to make exchanges as carefully or on the basis of as much information as their principals. In a world of many agents and few principals what might be conceived of as supervisory or policing costs may be so high that it is exceedingly difficult for principals to avoid inertia, carelessness and slothfulness on the part of agents.

The above should not be seen as a suggestion that all, or even most, agent–agent trading contractions will yield negative utility to both principals. The opposite may be true in the majority of cases. Of course, it is a matter of degree. But it raises an interesting and important research problem: What are the circumstances under which this happens to a greater rather than a lesser degree?

IV X-Efficiency Theory and Inert Areas

An important type of agent–agent exchange is the purchase of labour time by firms, which in turn leads to a pervasive phenomenon that I have referred to elsewhere as *X*-inefficiency.[1]

First, a word on its meaning: *X*-inefficiency is contrasted to allocative inefficiency. Inputs or factors of production may be allocated to the right units for use. However, there is no need to presume that the decision and performance entities involved must use inputs as effectively as possible. We refer to the difference between maximal effectiveness of the utilisation of inputs and the actual effectiveness as the degree of *X*-inefficiency. For present purposes it is of little importance whether we define this in terms of an absolute amount, or as a ratio. For instance, one possible ratio measure would be the deviation from maximal effectiveness as the numerator and the amount of maximal effectiveness as the denominator.

Thus, as the writer has argued in the past, it is one thing to allocate the inputs to productive entities, but it is a completely different matter to *use* such inputs 'efficiently'. Input utilisation involves many complexities. However, for purposes of this brief sketch, utilisation in terms of *time* and pace will suffice. For example, compare around-the-clock with hours-per-day operations; the allocation of manpower to factories, and the allocation of machines to these factories, will not be sufficient to determine the output that results. If effort is measured in time then the time and pace of use of the labour and equipment will be critical. Will the time and pace decisions be based on elements internal to the firm or on external considerations? Suppose that time use and pace are not given or determined by market conditions. In that case we would have to understand the internal organisation of our economic units and the responsiveness of internal components to external influences in order to understand the degree of *X*-efficiency which results.

In what follows we present very briefly, for what it is worth, the bare bones of a model under which the internal components of the firm respond to internal *non-market* conditions and external market conditions so that some degree of *X*-inefficiency emerges as a result. There is only room to outline salient features but none (unfortunately) to defend basic ideas.

(1) *Individual equilibrium*

Extremely detailed supervision is presumed to involve excessively high costs. Jobs are incompletely prescribed. Hence each individual who joins a firm *interprets* his job. An interpretation is a subset of *APQT* bundles (where A = *activities*, P = *pace*, Q = *quality*, and T is a composite of time duration and time *sequence* of activities). We refer to a specific *APQT* bundle as an *effort point* – a specific time sequence of activities carried out at a specific pace and at a given quality level. In general, an interpretation will involve a subset of adjacent or closely connected effort points which we refer to as an *effort position.* Thus a position allows an individual to move from one effort point to another in response to what he perceives as *legitimate* demands on his effort capacity. An individual is said to be in effort equilibrium if his effort point is in his *inert area.*

(2) *Inert areas*

The idea of inert areas is basic to the theory of the existence of *X*-inefficiency. The idea presumes that there is a utility cost of moving *out* of any position. Thus we conceive of an optimal inert area within which the utility cost of moving is greater than the utility gain. This is illustrated in Figure 1. The curve A represents the utility values of effort points from the agent's viewpoint. The curve *P* is the utility values of possible effort points for A from the viewpoint of *P*, the principal. The optimal inert area of A is the distance *I* on the ordinate bounded by the lines u_1 and u_2. Now, the actual effort position E_1 chosen by A is less than his optimal effort level E_2, and considerably less than the optimal effort level from the principal's viewpoint, E_3. Thus, the difference between E_1 and E_3 signifies *X*-inefficiency.

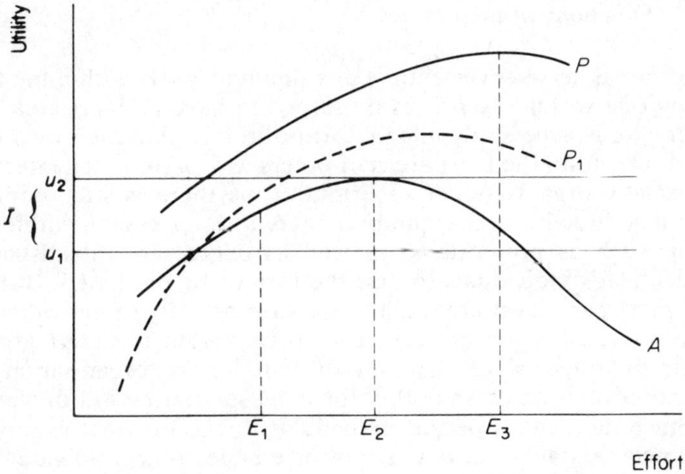

FIG. 1

It is of special interest to interpret the curve P_1 as representing the utility function of an agent-manager rather than that of the principal. Call the initial agent A_1 and the superior A_2. It is the basic characteristic of organisations that do not operate within markets that they must be hierarchical for purposes of communication and control. Thus the principal in general will be at the highest level of the hierarchy while agents exist on the lower rungs. It seems likely that, as a general case, the lower the rung on the hierarchy on which an agent exists, the greater the inert area he will have for his subordinates. Let us return for a moment to the difference between principal–principal trade and agent–agent trade. If, in principal–principal trade, one of the principals buys from another a specific piece of work to be accomplished on a one-off basis he will have a strong incentive to see that work is performed in accordance with his conception of the initial trade agreement. On the other hand, if it is an agent, say at the fifth rung of the hierarchical ladder, who hires someone to work at the sixth rung, he may have a very high degree of tolerance as to how the lower-level agent performs. The principal might not have purchased the labour time of the agent hired in the first place, or if he did he might very well have 'sold' (that is dismissed the employee) the labour time whereas the agent has no such strong incentive. It is not *his* money that is involved. Hence agent–agent trade in which the purchase of unspecified variable amounts of effort is likely to be a considerable source of X-inefficiency.

(3) *Functions of inert areas*

Inert areas serve several functions simultaneously within the firm. Everyone within the firm is presumed to have an inert area. Not everyone is necessarily in an effort position within their own inert area, or within the inert areas of others with whom they interact – especially organisational superiors. Thus there is still room for conflict, individual disequilibria, and for movement within the firm (such as promotions) as well as degrees of dissatisfaction which leads individuals to quit the firm or be dismissed. But, for the most part, inert areas allow the vast majority of individuals to find an equilibrium position and to be within the inert area of their 'interactees' so that, on the whole, the organisation can function reasonably smoothly for a substantial period of time.

Since inert areas permit individuals to choose what eventually becomes a stable effort position, it enables other individuals to develop reasonable expectations as to how various firm members will normally behave. It is such expectations which are usually required if there is to be a stable and meaningful demand and supply of effort in what is essentially a non-market context. The inert areas also operate as a lubricating agent within the firm since it allows for relatively loose fits between individual activities and what are presumed to be the firm's goals. Thus the very elements that contribute to stable performance and comfortable interaction are simultaneously the elements that allow for various degrees of X-inefficiency to be tolerated.

(4) *Effort, energy, entropy and competition*

A concept closely related to the effort positions of individuals is *effort entropy*. We presume that the effort positions are chosen within the constraints of incentives determined not only by supervisors and managers at higher levels in a hierarchy but also by the reaction of peers. There are various degrees to which management imposes constraints and presents incentives. If the constraints atrophy and the incentives for the pursuit of management objectives are attenuated, then we should expect some individuals to gradually shift their positions as they feel the loosening of constraints. It is such shifts in the direction of a reduction in the connectedness of effort points to 'firm objectives' that we designate as effort entropy. This is a latent process in all firms and organisations.

The process is likely to come about through two considerations: On the one hand the effort position will contain effort points which are closely connected to the managerial interpretation of the firm's objectives. As constraints and incentives atrophy the individual is less likely to feel demands for the more connected effort points and will shift gradually to the less connected ones. In addition, as external constraints appear to recede in importance the individual will have a new conception of the effort–utility relation illustrated in Figure 1 (p. 61). As a result what was previously an effort position within an inert area may now turn out to be one outside it, and individuals will move to positions which improve their new conception of utility from effort but which simultaneously have a lesser connection with perceived firm objectives. Thus, one of the functions of management and entrepreneurship is to struggle against the latent effort entropy in order to avoid increases in cost.

The process we have just considered has some interesting alternative implications for competition versus monopoly as market structures. In the conventional theory both competitive firms and monopolistic firms are presumed to minimise costs. Therefore, other things being equal, cost levels are assumed to be the same for monopolies and competitive firms. In this model no such presumption is made. We expect that normally monopolistic managements will not have the incentive to struggle against effort entropy to the same extent as competitive firms. The lesser struggle against entropy by monopolists and the higher unit costs can be made up by the monopoly's capacity to charge higher prices for its goods. Under competition there is a severely limited degree to which any particular firm can raise its price in response to its own increase in costs. As a result, staying within certain cost levels becomes a matter of survival itself under competition. Hence we should expect that surviving firms under competition will have a much stronger incentive to struggle against effort entropy than under monopoly.

The implications of the above for the welfare-loss estimation under monopoly is illustrated in the highly simplified diagram in Figure 2. Constant costs with respect to scale are assumed. The price under monopoly is P_m. Unit costs are *Bb* under monopoly and competition if *X*-inefficiency is excluded. However, if our calculation includes the *X*-efficiency effect so that competition also involves a lower cost of production (as shown by *Cc*) then the welfare loss also includes the additional production cost under monopoly. This is equal to *BbcC*. It is readily apparent that

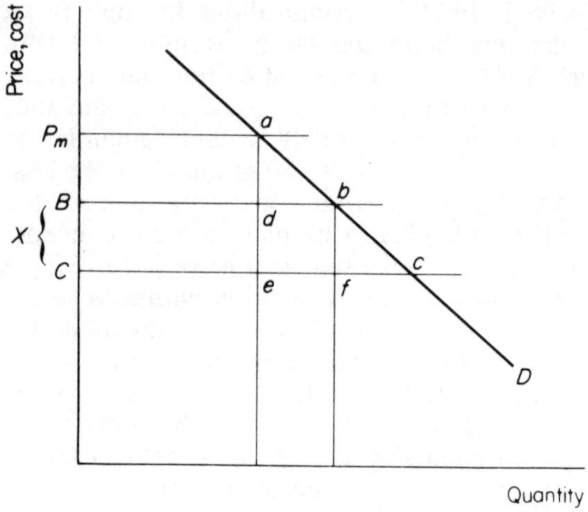

FIG. 2

if the cost difference between monopoly and competition is equal to or larger than the price mark-up under monopoly, then the order of magnitude of the welfare loss attributable to the cost differential is likely to be very much greater than that which merely results from the fact that the monopoly price is higher than the competitive one. This can increase the significance of monopoly as a contributor to welfare loss if the X-efficiency effect is included.[2]

(6) *Competitive equilibrium*

Although we argued that monopoly is likely to result in a greater degree of X-inefficiency than would competition we should not presume that there would be an absence of X-inefficiency under competitive equilibrium. In this model of the competitive process, pressure to lower cost is a consequence of the expansion rate and the cost reductions achieved by existing firms, the rate of entry and the cost levels of entering firms, compared to the latent gradual rise in costs due to effort entropy. Thus we may visualise that the equilibrium will be struck in part by the interaction of the effort entropy effect which tends to raise costs and the entry-expansion effect which puts pressure on firms to lower costs. The outcome under competition may readily contain a considerable degree of X-inefficiency, depending on the degree of entrepreneurial sluggishness in entering an industry.

V Some Unorthodox Iso-Value Curves

Iso-value curves are common tools of geometrical treatments of economic theory, or of geometrical illustrations of more mathematical formulations. The normal assumption is that such iso-value curves, such as isoquants or indifference curves, are convex from below. In this section I want to indicate briefly that, once effort is a variable, indirect influences between inputs can result in some rather unorthodox-looking iso-value curves that may have some explanatory potential.

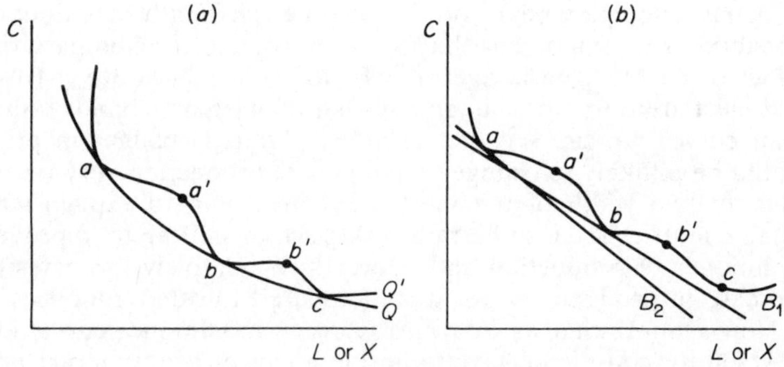

FIG. 3

Consider the normal isoquant of production theory illustrated by the curve Q in Figure 3. The axes C and L represent units of capital and labour time. Now if effort is variable then it is possible for the capital employed to influence the effort put forth within a given amount of labour time through its effect on organisational factors, and thus indirectly to influence the rate of substitutability of capital for labour as we increase capital and decrease labour. Suppose we move from the point b to the point a in the illustration. In the conventional treatment we would assume that there is a diminishing marginal rate of substitutability as capital is substituted for labour. Hence the usual convex shape of the curve is derived. But suppose that capital is 'effort stretching'. If the degree of effort stretching is sufficiently great then up to a point we should expect an increasing rate of substitutability of capital for labour and the isoquant would take on the shape as in Q' which contains increasing rate of substitutability (concave) segments. We do not have the space to examine all the possible implications and interpretations of curves such as Q'. However, it should be readily apparent that in the neighbourhood of the points *a*, *b* and *c* small changes in price could result in very limited changes in the capital–labour ratio, but slightly larger changes in relative price could result in an extreme jump in the production technique – the kind of jump that would not occur with the usual convex isoquants. This might help to explain two types of phenomena which are frequently observed: (1) fairly similar styles of production in similar industries in different countries despite the fact that relative input prices are different; and (2) the shift to relatively capital-intensive modes of production in some industries in the urban sector of developing countries in the face of urban unemployment and despite the '*physically*' continuous possibilities of equipment that could be produced. (Compare the effect of a shift from budget line B_1 to B_2 in Figure 3(*b*).) If we add inert areas to our isoquants so that they become bands rather than curves we can see that relatively limited changes in price would be unlikely to change techniques of production very much. The relative width of the inert areas may help to explain why some countries seem to be rather sluggish in shifting to improved techniques of production and hence show relatively low rates of increase in productivity per man compared to other countries.

Now suppose that we interpret Q' as an indifference curve. Let C stand for conspicuous consumption goods or 'status goods' and X stand for ordinary 'non-status' consumption goods. The points a' and b' would not be observed. The implication is that households care about the external aspects of their life-styles and the social status image that it implies. Thus if prices and income allows a household to live at point *a* it would do so, but otherwise it would shift to choice *b* and ignore the alternatives in between since these do not reflect a distinctive style. Essentially the point made is that, from a physical viewpoint, consumption mixes may be continuous but from a psychological one they are distinctive, and frequently households will attempt to purchase bundles of goods clustered around the distinctive life-style or status image they are just able to afford.

If in addition to the above we introduce the inert-area idea so that the indifference curves become bands then we can readily see that small changes in income would shift the budget line within the band and not change the life-style very much. This suggests that a certain degree of stickiness to distinctive life-style consumption standards will generally be observed.

VI Final Remarks

We have presented in outline form some relatively new approaches to micro theory. Basic elements in the views stressed are inertia (as interpreted by inert areas), interpersonal relationships as elements that lead to non-optimal behaviour both on the individual and group levels. Such behaviour on the individual level leads to the non-optimal behaviour of the traditional economic units, the firm and the household. These notions may help us to analyse differences in the X-efficiency of firms, industries, and economies. Unless we can capture the sources of various degrees of inertia or sluggishness that exist in economies, and unless we can find tools for analysing such conditions, then our capacity to understand changing economic conditions of various countries are likely to be severely limited.

We do not have the space to go into the relationship between degrees of inertia and related tools of analysis, but these modes of thought can be used to analyse the introduction of innovations and the different degrees with which the diffusion of such innovations take place.[3] The reverse side of the innovation coin is resistance to change and the location of size of inert areas helps to explain this phenomenon. It is hoped that the further development of such ideas may help us to analyse the alterations of growth spurts and depressed phases that have characterised the behaviour of both developed and developing countries in the last three decades. The analysis of such phenomena are especially significant in a world in which agents rather than principals make many of the important economic decisions.

Some readers will no doubt have noticed some overlap between some of the ideas presented above and those of the 'Carnegie School.[4] One of the interesting questions which arises in this connection is why the Carnegie School's ideas never really made much headway – at least it seems that way at the time of writing. The new approaches suggested by members of that school have not been incorporated in the usual textbooks at the various levels, nor in the normal curricula through which economists are trained. While many reasons can be put forward as to why this should have occurred (for example, it has been argued that it is a rather incomplete theory – just bits and pieces of theorising), Cohen and Cyert quite accurately classify these theories as 'new approaches' to the theory of the firm rather than as full-fledged alternatives to neoclassical theory.

A reason that comes to mind (and one whose importance it would be difficult to underestimate) is that new ideas have a tough baptism if they are outside the modes of thought used by economists for over a century – a mode of thinking which recurs in infinite varieties in microeconomics. Essentially it is an optimising view of behaviour at almost every level. It is as though the economic profession has a fixation with optimisation as a description of the behaviour of firms and households. As a consequence, notions which depart from this general mode, or which cannot readily be absorbed into it, are initially or ultimately ignored. In the last analysis, one has to face the question whether actual behaviour is better described through some optimisation decision-making process or through alternative modes of thought.

Even if empirical studies prove, to the extent possible, that non-optimising behaviour by individuals and groups fits the facts better than the current alternative, this does not imply that we must choose between theories once and for all. Most likely there is a need for both types of theories. There may be a class of problems under which the abstractions from reality characterised by maximising (or optimising) behaviour assumptions may be useful. The simplicity of these theories is frequently a virtue in analysis. However, there may be a large class of other problems where models and theories which are based on non-optimising behaviour can give superior results. There is no reason to look at these matters in terms of either/or choices.

Finally, what I have referred to as micro–micro theory is part of the researchable frontier. However, we are probably putting unnecessary obstacles in our way if we continue to be bewitched by the mathematics and logic of optimisation as vehicles for describing behaviour rather than examining theories on the basis of empirical considerations. In any event at this late stage in the development of microeconomic theory it appears to be both interesting and possibly useful to experiment with new approaches.

4 Economic Dynamics and Economic Policy

Sir Roy Harrod

The system of traditional economics may be called a static one. It was concerned with the interrelation of the supply, demand and prices of commodities and factors of production at a given point of time.

The system of J. M. Keynes was also static. Where he departed from the traditional classical system was not in introducing a dynamic element but in analysing aggregate demand. The traditional school assumed that the sum total of demands for the various goods and services would be sufficient (and no more than sufficient) to give full employment. Keynes showed that total demands would not necessarily be of this amount; they might be insufficient to give full employment or they might be greater than enough to give full employment thereby setting up a demand-pull inflation. Incidentally, Keynes only gave a passing reference to the possibility of a cost-push inflation; but the serious inflations from which most important countries have suffered in recent years have been cost-push inflations. These inflations have proceeded concurrently with quite serious unemployment. This has been paradoxical from the points of view both of the old traditional and of what is called Keynesian economics.

Economic dynamics is concerned with an entirely different set of relations. The question is often raised whether someone is a neoclassical or a Keynesian economist. So far as statics is concerned, it is the case that the great majority of competent economists are Keynesian. The so-called neoclassicals are a rather small eccentric group. But Keynes's systematic theory as expounded in the 1930s does not include a dynamic element.

The system of economic dynamics, or, as one may call it, the theory of economic growth, may be introduced by setting out the most fundamental equation. One may first consider it in the form of an axiom that is necessarily true, that is

$$G = \frac{s}{C},$$

where G stands for the growth rate of the economy, s for the fraction of income (= output) saved and C for the capital–output ratio, that is the amount of capital required to produce a unit of output. This equation may be related to any unit of time. It is convenient to take a year as the unit of time by which to assess the rate of growth.

One may next proceed to what may be called an equilibrium growth equation, that is

$$G_w = \frac{s_d}{C_r}.$$

Here s_d stands for the fraction of income that people (including companies) desire to save. What they actually save may deviate from this from time to time (upwards or downwards). In a boom companies may find themselves receiving more profit than they need to set aside for further expansion. In due course they will doubtless distribute this to their shareholders. Then the shareholders, finding their incomes enlarged, will spend part of the increase on additional consumption. It is assumed that persons will have definite ideas about what fractions of their income they wish to save. When their incomes increase, they will normally both spend and save more. C_r stands for the amount of capital needed for a unit increase of output. The equilibrium equation shows what the rate of growth, G_w, is when persons and companies are saving the fraction of income they wish to save and the additions to capital are what are required most conveniently to produce the extra output. Given the fraction of extra income that companies and persons wish to save and given the capital–output ratio, there is one growth rate that is consistent with this. It is shown in the equation by G_w. By way of example one might take the desired saving ratio to be 10 per cent and the capital–output ratio as 3; this, in accordance with the equation, would give a growth rate of 3·3 per cent per annum.

The peculiarity of this growth equation is that it gives an unstable position. In this it is unlike the equations of static economics. If the amount of a commodity, say wheat, that is produced causes the price of that commodity to fall below its cost of production, then there will be a tendency for less to be produced. The marginal producers, namely those whose costs are highest, will curtail their output or go out of business. So long as there is what may be called 'excess' production the level of production will tend to fall. Conversely, if production is below the equilibrium level prices will tend to stand above the marginal cost of production and these will cause more to be produced. Thus there is a tendency for the price to move to its equilibrium level. In cases of monopoly, or partial monopoly, the equilibrium level may tend to be above the marginal cost of production. The underlying forces of supply and demand remain, and equilibrium is a stable one, in the sense that deviations from it will be followed by reversions back to it.

An equilibrium position may be accompanied by unemployment. The old view was that there would be a tendency for this unemployment to disappear in due course. It was thought that unemployment would cause people to offer their goods and services at lower prices and that this would increase the amount of the goods and services demanded. This seems to imply free competition in the markets for goods and services. In fact, monopoly or quasi-monopoly has for long been present in the markets for many goods and services, for example in the existence of trade unions. This is not the fundamental explanation of unemployment. There was much unemployment in the nineteenth century when the trade unions were still very weak. We have to revert to the equilibrium growth equation. If the value of G_w, as determined by the equation, is below the growth that would occur if the economy was fully employed, there will be unemployment.

Next it must be noted that the equilibrium shown by the equation is an unstable one. If the actual G is at any time in excess of G_w, then s must be greater than desired s, or C must be smaller than desired C, or both. If people find that they are saving more than they desire to, they will increase their orders for current goods and services. Thus, if actual G is running above the equilibrium G_w this will tend to increase G, that is raise it still further above the equilibrium level. If C is below the required level, this will cause an increase of orders on capital account and, likewise, will tend to raise actual G. On this account, too, there will be an acceleration of growth. The departure from equilibrium will be cumulative. At some point a ceiling of full employment, or one may call it over-full employment, will be reached, at which the high rate of growth can no longer be maintained. This will cause a relapse. There will be a cumulative downward movement. Thus we have the alternation of boom and slump, which has been so characteristic of the capitalist system ever since the Industrial Revolution. In earlier days, when there was much less hired labour, the matter was different. The mass of people owned their own plots of land or were serfs whose masters made them go on working at something or other – to improve their property, and so forth.

The system is also unstable in a downward direction. If actual growth is below the equilibrium level, either people will be saving less than they desire to or the capital–output ratio will be greater than what is required, and in either case there will be a downward movement of aggregate demand. This will push actual growth still further away from its equilibrium level.

Next we may frame the concept of 'natural' (or optimum) rate of growth. This is the rate of growth that causes the aggregate demand for goods and services to be neither above nor below the potential supply of the economy. Allowance must of course be made for frictional unemployment, as caused by the need for those employed in some particular production centre, the activity of which is being reduced, to look around for another employer, or to change their trade, or even migrate to another part of the country. We have the equation

$$G_\sigma = \frac{s_\sigma}{C_r},$$

where the suffix σ denotes 'optimal'.

In the equilibrium equation it is assumed that people and companies are free to save just the amount that they wish to. It is their free choice about how much to save that determines the equilibrium growth rate. But if we assume that growth is sustained at the level of which the economy is capable, as defined above, then the fraction that people and companies collectively have to save is determined. They can no longer save in accordance with their self-interest or whims. Collectively they have to save what is required. It may be expedient to alter the order of the symbols. In the equilibrium equation the growth rate was the *determinand* and put on the left-hand side; in the optimal equation it is the fraction of income saved that is the *determinand*. One may show this by putting s_σ on the left-hand side, that is

$$s_\sigma = G_\sigma \,.\, C_r.$$

The actual growth rate may have no tendency to equal the optimal growth rate. This is the fundamental reason that makes economic planning desirable. The determination by a number of countries after the Second World War to have full employment was responsible for the great increase in economic planning. The old-fashioned doubtless thought that the way to ensure full employment was to prevent excessive increases of wages. This was not practicable at the time and was, in fact, theoretically incorrect. Holding wages down would not secure full employment, if the equilibrium growth rate, as determined by the fraction of income saved and the capital–output ratio, was not such as to give a growth rate at the optimal level. If the growth as determined by the desire to save and the capital–output ratio was below the optimal growth rate then the public authorities would have to supplement the demand for productive resources by instituting public works or using their authority to insist on capital reconstruction in certain industries.

An economic planning agency has two traditional weapons, namely monetary and fiscal policy. The monetary weapon inevitably has an influence on interest rates. Tight money is associated with high interest and vice versa.

The old traditional classical view was that the rate of interest was governed by the supply of and demand for saving. Keynes made a break here with his doctrine that the economy was not always necessarily at its full-employment level. The supply of saving would be different according to the level of economic activity in the economy and, indeed, it might constitute a different fraction of the national income according to the state of the economy. Keynes's own special doctrine was that the actual rate of interest depended on the supply of, and demand for, liquidity. This had some plausibility. In dynamic theory, however, interest should figure as a function of the growth rate. One would also have to consider whether the equilibrium position would be one of a rate of interest rising or falling through time. In practice, this would hardly be a workable theory as, if the rate was to continue to move in one direction, its change in a finite period of moderate length, such as a year, would have to be very small indeed and this would be quite inconsistent with the normal ups and downs of the stock exchanges.

It is needful to consider the intrinsic character of interest. The basic case for the existence of interest is the diminishing marginal utility of income through time. If the income and consumption per head in an economy are growing, the representative person usually expects the marginal utility of consumption at some future point of time to be less than it is at present. Accordingly, if he is asked to sacrifice present consumption in return for the availability of means for some extra consumption in the future, in short to make a loan, he needs some compensation for the lower marginal utility of the purchasing power that he obtains when the corpus of the loan is paid back to him. That compensation constitutes interest. In practice, there must be some haziness about the rate at which the income of the representative person will grow in the time ahead and, therefore, about the rate of interest that is appropriate.

There are, doubtless, some individuals who expect their incomes to fall through time, and it would be advantageous for these to save even if they received no interest at all. But, on a weighted average, such people are in a minority in a progressive economy. Such as they would make without the inducement of interest would not usually be sufficient to satisfy the net capital requirements of the community.

Accordingly, banking policy should be framed so as to cause the interest rate to move to the optimal level. This maxim does not, in fact, give the banking system much guidance, owing to the uncertainty about what the rate of growth of income will be and what the current optimum rate of interest in fact is. But the criterion does set limits. Control over aggregate demand by the monetary weapon designed to secure full employment and optimum growth might entail interest rates that are obviously too low or obviously too high in relation to the aforementioned criterion. It is for this reason that monetary policy for controlling aggregate demand should be supplemented by fiscal policy. In principle, the mix of monetary policy and fiscal policy that ought to be put into effect to control aggregate demand is not a matter that can in principle be left to the convenience of administrators or politicians but should be such that monetary management provides the optimum rate of interest by the criterion defined above.

The correct management of aggregate demand should be such as to ensure full employment and expansion at a maintainable rate. If the optimum rate of interest is very low it may be necessary to mop up excess purchasing power by surpluses in the budgets of public expenditure and vice versa.

It has been often supposed that with aggregate demand maintained at this level and not allowed to rise above this level there will be no inflation. This rests on the view that the existence of inflation is always caused by an excess of aggregate demand over the supply potential of the economy. This view is not tenable. It is possible for there to be inflation, and indeed this very frequently happens, when aggregate demand is not in excess of the supply potential of the economy. To prevent the occurrence of inflation an extra weapon is needed.

We have seen that there are two weapons by which the maintenance of aggregate demand at the right level can be maintained, namely monetary and fiscal policies. But the correct use of these two weapons will not necessarily, or even probably, prevent the occurrence of inflation. This is where there has been an important development of economic theory in recent years. Inflation will occur if increases in rates of pay are greater than increases in productivity. The idea that this will never happen so long as aggregate demand is not in excess of the supply potential is not tenable.

To achieve the objective of preventing inflation we need, not necessarily always, an extra weapon, namely direct interference with the course of wages and prices. We have had such direct interferences rather frequently in recent times. There is a widespread belief that such interferences are something abnormal, that they are due to recent aberrations in monetary and fiscal policies that have allowed aggregate demand to mount too high, and will not be needed if monetary and fiscal policies are appropriately conducted. This is incorrect. If it is asked why direct interference has not seemed to be needed before, the answer is that we have a new target of policy, namely the level of employment. In the old days employment was supposed to be able to look after itself and not require government supervision; however the bad bouts of unemployment that have occurred cannot be attributed to excessive deflation.

If we take a somewhat longer historical view we find that rates of increase of wages and prices did not look after themselves. For many centuries in the United Kingdom these rates were supervised by the Justices of the Peace and there have been similar interferences in other countries.

We have next to consider foreign trade. There will be an optimum in relation to the net amount of capital exported or imported by a given country. We may start by assuming that there is no international capital movement so that a country's exports of goods and services must be equal to its imports. Exports and imports will both have a specific content as determined by the law of comparative costs. A given country of marked efficiency may be able to produce all tradeable goods at a lower real cost than can its trading partners. One has a schedule of comparative efficiencies in respect of all the various goods. The highly efficient country will export goods in which her comparative advantage is greater, and import goods in which her comparative advantage is less. She will import certain goods even if in real terms she could produce them more efficiently, that is at lower real costs than her trading partners. The various components of the exports and imports will have their own growth rates. As the world grows richer its demands for the various objects do not grow at the same rate. It may happen that the average of the world's demand for the goods that a given country exports grows more slowly than the average of its own demands for the goods that it imports. In that case, if we start from a point at which the country's foreign trade is in balance, it will develop a growing external trade deficit. What should be the remedy?

Those at the theoretical end of these considerations are inclined to say that the remedy for an imbalance should be a change in the foreign exchange rate. A difficulty about this is that it creates uncertainty, which is bad for the development of trade. As trade expands more and more traders are involved in long-term contracts, and, in order to evaluate these, they need to know what the exchange rate will be.

Strictly speaking, within the context of a growth theory, one should envisage a steady movement, one way or another, in the rate of exchange. This would hardly be practicable as dealers anticipate the future and the balance of their supply and demand would probably lead not to a steadier moving rate but to rather frequent jumps in the rate. It could be argued that these matters can be dealt with by the purchase and sale of forward exchange. But the forward markets do not provide facilities stretching over a rather long period ahead. An attempt to do so would lead to severe complications. Nor would traders always use such facilities even if they existed. It might not be in their interest to do so. For instance, take the case of an importer, the currency of whose country is deemed by the traders as, on the whole, likely to appreciate; if their view is correct, then the importer would do well not to take advantage of the facilities provided by a forward market. If he buys the needed currency forward he will buy it at a rate that is not very far removed from the current spot rate. But if the idea that there will be appreciation is correct, then he will get his imports more cheaply by not buying foreign currency spot or forward immediately, but by buying it only when he has to make the payment.

One must suppose that, even with a fluctuating rate, there will be some official intervention in order to secure a reasonable amount of steadiness. Some theorists talk of a freely floating rate, and this expedient has occasionally been adopted. But usually a free float would lead to excessive oscillations. Official intervention has to be based on judgement; there cannot be hard and fast rules for the guidance of the authorities.

The occurrence of imbalances in external trade may be due to seasonal, cyclical or structural causes. The authorities have to judge which of these causes is responsible for a given imbalance; more than one of these types of cause may be operating at a given point of time. It might be claimed that it should be possible to identify at least the seasonal causes, but this may not always be so. Crop variations may give rise to seasonal discrepancies of different sizes as between one season and another. The authorities would have to assess this. Again it is partly a matter of judgement.

Cyclical variations produce much more difficult problems. Trade cycles do not occur with a perfectly uniform rhythm. The study of economic history shows this clearly. Cycles have varied greatly both in their amplitude and in their duration. Once again, and still more so in this case, the authorities responsible for exchange-rate policy would be confronted with problems of great complexity.

There is a more fundamental difficulty. A devaluation does not necessarily improve the external balance of the country that undertakes it. It will not do so if the elasticities of the supply and demand of the goods entering into foreign trade are low. The recognised formula is that the sum of the elasticities of the supply of exports and the demand for imports must be greater than one. Much recent experience has suggested rather low elasticities. At this the theorists interpose with the proposition that it is the short-period elasticities that are sometimes low and that it is highly probable that the sum of the long-term elasticities will be greater than one. There is a whiff of dogmatism in this. It is not always certain to be the case with the long-term elasticities, and of course these are more difficult to assess than the short-term elasticities. It is difficult not to have the idea that the theorists make these assertions because they are determined to have things their own way. They are devotees of the theory that appropriate foreign-exchange-rate variations are bound to bring matters to rights. It is difficult to formulate precisely what the findings of experience are, since many other relevant changes are occurring simultaneously with the exchange-rate changes.

Admittedly in some cases the desirability of a change may be obvious, as when a country has had a large across-the-board inflation considerably in excess of the inflations occurring among its trading partners. But imbalances of trade are by no means confined to such cases. It is to be noted that if devaluation is judged to be the correct remedy for some countries, and if these countries were deemed to have a right to devalue in the circumstances, this should be complemented by the idea that it is the duty of countries in structural surplus to value their currencies upwards. Over a wide range of moral theory rights are deemed to be complemented by duties. If the world authorities, whoever they may be, are permissive in regard to devaluations in certain circumstances, then they should be strict in insisting that surplus countries value upwards. Upward valuations should collectively be of the same order of magnitude as devaluations. If they are not, then the world as a whole will be the victim of spiralling inflation.

What is actually done is bound to depend in part on the attitudes of the authorities of the countries concerned. These attitudes are conditioned by the pressures to which the country is subject. The trouble is that if a country is in continuing deficit, it is under strong pressure to do something about it. If it fails to do so, then in due course its reserve will be exhausted. By contrast a surplus country can just sit back and do nothing to remedy its surplus. Money will continue to flow in; well, the country concerned may judge that this is very nice. Indifference to its own surplus may be human and natural, but the fact remains that it is unneighbourly.

There is another possible weapon for coping with an external deficit, namely the restriction of imports, whether by protection or tariffs or by direct controls. Theorists strongly object to such expedients although in fact they are widely used. If the case for an exchange-rate change is not clear – and the great difficulties confronting a diagnosis have been pointed out above – then import restriction should be employed. They are superior to an exchange-rate change, unless the latter is manifestly desirable;

they can be selective. They can be imposed in the first instance on unnecessary luxuries. A devaluation means that imports become more expensive across the board, and these imports may contain important necessities of life. They may also include raw materials that enter into the cost of producing exports. Import restrictions are definitely superior to deflation as a remedy for an external imbalance, unless, of course, the country is suffering from domestic-demand inflation. There may often be an external imbalance owing to the changing composition of the marginal needs of a growing country without there being any domestic-demand inflation at all. Indeed the country may be suffering from very sizeable unemployment. Unless aggregate demand is excessive in a country, that is above the full-employment level, reducing demand creates unemployment. In terms of human welfare, unemployment is a far greater evil than being cut off from the power to purchase imports that are not strictly necessary.

The international capital flow must next be considered. In economic statics this is a negative item in the external balance of payments. In economic dynamics the opposite is the case. In statics we analyse the equilibrium and the various relations at a given point of time. In dynamics we have to consider a continuing flow. The analysis may still be concerned with a given point of time, but a before and an after are also involved. There is the familiar analogy with a railway train. It may be stationary, and statics is concerned with the stresses in its various parts. But if it is moving, change is proceeding. At a given point of time it is altering its position at a certain rate. It may be travelling at a uniform velocity or it may be accelerating. Economic dynamics are concerned with the mutual relations of the growth (or shrinkage) of the various parts of the system. There were strong dynamic elements in the writing of the early classical economists. But interest in these was lost later in the nineteenth century, and the attention of those in the vanguard of economics was centered on the static interconnections of an economy.

In the case of international capital flow at a given point of time, or, more realistically, in a finite period of time, we have a given amount of capital invested abroad and we have an inflow from capital previously invested. With steady progress the outflow in a given year will be smaller than the inflow of returns on capital investment abroad. Our basic dynamic analysis should be concerned with the continuing process. Of course, there may be discontinuities. A country which has not previously made capital investment abroad may start doing so. Then for a time the value of its capital outflow will be greater than the value of the inflow from its capital invested abroad. This would also be the case if a country made a discontinuous increase of substantial size in the capital that it invested abroad. Such discontinuities have to be considered. But the fundamental equations of dynamic theory should express the interrelations between continuing flows. These can be further elaborated to cover the case of steadily accelerating or decelerating flows. It may be noted that in the decades before 1914 the United Kingdom was of all countries in the world by far the largest investor of capital abroad, but the yield in each given year from capital previously invested abroad was greater than the amount of capital thus invested. In recent times some less-developed nations, like India, have been resistant to foreign capital investment in their territories. It has been widely averred that this has been due to nationalism in these countries and their unwillingness to give foreigners the power to dictate to them in a way that foreign capital investment within their borders would entail. That may indeed have been one motive for their attitude, but a far more important motive, clearly understood by the Indians, was appreciation that such foreign investment would constitute a net burden on their balance of payments.

In economic dynamics it is quite evident that the investment of capital abroad is a favourable item in a country's balance of payments and an unfavourable one in the balances of the countries receiving the capital.

There is a big time lag between what is learnt at a university in economics by ministers or civil servants and their arrival into positions of power where they can influence events. When in power they are apt to think in terms of what they learnt when they were young. The matter is different in the case of the natural sciences, where those working on projects of the applied sciences just have to know the latest findings of university laboratories. High-up administrators at the present time (1976) have largely learnt their economics from such economists as Walras, Alfred Marshall and A. C. Pigou and their disciples. These were all 'static' economists. Alfred Marshall did indeed set his hand to writing a fourth volume planned to incorporate economic-growth theory, but by that time he was already too old and the notes that he prepared for it made little sense.

The present administrators do not, for the most part, realise that there has come into being a new branch of economics, which we may call economic dynamics or the economics of growth, one that contains a whole system of axioms and corollaries entirely different from anything to be found in the authors who wrote the prescribed texts for the universities some thirty years ago. Accordingly, it is important to lay stress on, and publicise, the fact that a new system of thought has come into being.

5 The Meaning and Validity of Institutional Economics*

Gunnar Myrdal

The dissenters from conventional economic theory have devoted the main part of their scholarly endeavours to analysing specific problems in regard to which they found this theory insufficient and faulty. But enough of us have from time to time taken up the general problem of why, how, and in what respects this conventional theory goes wrong and how an institutional theory, free from these systematic defects, should be shaped. As yet there are, however, no comprehensive treatises written by institutional economists where our thoughts on the whole range of economic problems have been systematised. But the concord among us in basic philosophy and approaches to theoretical and political questions is so great that even the task of writing institutional textbooks ought now to tempt some of our younger colleagues. The most fundamental thought that binds us together is our understanding that, in regard to practically every economic problem, scientific study must concern the entire social system, including, besides the so-called economic factors, everything else of importance for what comes to happen in the economic field. The reason why this is a methodological imperative is the fact that, among all conditions in that system, there is circular causation. This implies interdependence. A change in one condition will cause changes in other conditions which, in turn, will cause new

* The paper was originally prepared as an essay for a volume in honour of Professor K. William Kapp.

changes all around, and so forth. So the whole social system will be moving in one direction or another, and it may even then be turning around its axis. There is no basic cause, but everything causes everything else.

If, as an abstract supposition, the system were assumed to be at rest in an initial moment, then after a change there would be no equilibrium in sight. This is more particularly so because we know from empirical study that changes which are reactions to a more primary change often, though not always, tend to go in the same direction. Thus a rise in income for a group of people in a poor country will permit higher nutritional levels which, in turn, may increase labour productivity and incomes.

This is why circular causation normally will have cumulative effects. Through feedbacks causing more primary changes to have repercussions in the same direction, the reactions for good or ill may after some time be quite out of proportion to an initial impulse changing one or several conditions.

As the system is moving, the coefficients of interrelations among various conditions in circular causation are ordinarily not known with any precision. Elements of inertia, time lags, and in extreme cases the total non-responsiveness of one or several conditions to changes in some set of other conditions are problems of great complexity. This is largely true even in developed countries with their more complete analysis of all social conditions and their more perfected statistical services. But it is particularly true in under-developed countries. Consequently, our analysis of their development problems must often end in broad generalisations and merely plausible hypotheses, built upon limited observation, discernment and conjectural judgements. Even in developed countries a widening of perspective will regularly destroy the neat simplicity of both analyses and conclusions.

The above remarks are offered as hints toward the master model of the institutional approach, which in principle is holistic. It is founded upon logic. But to us institutional economists it is validated as a research methodology by the results we have been reaching when trying to follow it out.

In calling the holistic approach the fundamental principle of institutional economics, I imply that our main accusation against conventional economists is that they work with 'closed models' with too few variables. These are chosen from conditions called 'economic factors' which regularly are more susceptible to quantification, although even this quality is often opportunistically exaggerated, and not only in regard to under-developed countries.

Holding down the number of variables to only a few that can be quantified makes possible the use of impressive mathematical models. Such closed models regularly presuppose a sharp restriction of vision. Almost the entire social system is kept out of sight. This should at least have required a clear statement of assumptions with respect to conditions and determinants not considered. Such an account of implied assumptions is regularly not given, and I have never met an economist of the conventional brand who was really aware of that basic weakness of his analysis.

For reasons I have already alluded to, a more accomplished institutional analysis, not working with this wholesale exclusion of so much which is important, will seldom be able to argue quantitatively in such precise terms, simply because our knowledge of all relevant facts and the interrelations between those facts is not that precise.

However, it is certainly a mistake to accuse the institutional economists of presenting their analysis without many figures. This leads to a facile characterisation of our reasoning as 'qualitative' rather than quantitative. When we do not display figures so carelessly, it is because, trained to work with problems where facts are as yet not known in precise terms, we are generally more critical than conventional economists. But we are equally, or more, intent upon reaching quantified knowledge as soon and as broadly as possible.

Another mistake is to believe that we are hostile to theory and models. We just want our theory and models, indeed even the concepts we use, to be more adequate to the reality we are studying.

Already from the beginnings of the discipline in the eighteenth and early nineteenth centuries, economists unhesitatingly saw themselves as political economists. They firmly believed it was part of their duty to draw policy conclusions and to do so on rational grounds, that is as logical inferences from their knowledge about facts.

They stressed, however, that their 'theory' – the prototype of present-day conventional economists' closed models – was not itself broad enough to permit them to draw policy conclusions, but that in order to be able to do this, they had to add knowledge from a wider field, particularly assumptions from social philosophy. In the meaning already clarified by John Stuart Mill in his earliest works, the study of economic problems was a 'moral science'.

Crucial for this older view, which established economic science as political economy, was the conviction that there were objective values that could be known as facts, could be observed and analysed, and so utilised as the basis for a study of all other facts and for rational policy conclusions. This value basis for economic study was provided by the moral philosophy of that time, utilitarianism, based on the hedonistic associational psychology.

Though it cannot be pretended that institutional economists have always been clear on this point, I do believe that very generally it can be maintained that we have stuck to the old tradition of looking upon our work as political economy and our science as a moral science. Our inclination to do so is, of course, somewhat natural, because many of the leading economists in the classical and neoclassical tradition from Adam Smith to Alfred Marshall have been broader in their approaches than the conventional economists, particularly those in the era after the Second World War. Many of us have from time to time been tempted to include these wider-ranging forebears among our predecessors as institutional economists, together with writers in other lines like Friedrich List and Karl Marx.

But we have not been able to stick to the basis which the classical and neoclassical school sought in the moral philosophy of utilitarianism and the hedonistic associational psychology. And so we have been forced to attempt to find another valuational basis for our work than this obsolete philosophy and psychology. I have made it clear that we need to work with explicit instrumental value premises, which should be relevant and significant in the society studied, logically consistent in their own right, and feasible for potential realisation.

With that methodological problem I have been living all my life as a student of economics. I cannot speak for the institutional economists as a group, except to assert that we are all political economists, and therefore have all been involved in the problems of how to account for the role of human valuations in research and in policy prescriptions. Like our predecessors outside the classical and neoclassical schools, we have had our eyes open for resultant biases in research when valuational assumptions are concealed, while the very idea of that type of opportunistic distortion is almost a forbidden thought in conventional economics.

About the problem of the role of valuations in research, the conventional economists have managed to preserve an almost complete naivete. They have retained the welfare theory developed by the last generation of neoclassical authors but have succeeded in concealing and forgetting its foundation in a particular and now obsolete moral philosophy and an equally obsolete psychology. They have pursued what appears to be an amoral and apsychological economic theory, and they are proud to stress the result as 'professionalism' – hence keeping their theory 'pure'.

Hundreds of books and articles are produced every year on 'welfare economics'. But if the approach is not entirely meaningless, it has a meaning only through a forlorn hedonistic psychology and a utilitarian moral philosophy. To this is related the reluctance of conventional economists to study, empirically and in terms of modern psychology, people's behaviour as income earners, consumers, savers and investors. I have long been pointing to the unsatisfactory relation between conventional economics and modern psychology.

Conventional economists apparently assume that they can study human behaviour without caring how it is caused. In practice, this amounts to preserving – while often explicitly disavowing – the hedonistic assumptions that human behaviour is rational in weighing 'utilities' and 'disutilities', without accounting for how such rationality is supposedly achieved. The result is a general tendency towards a very particular bias, pretending market rationality and optimality, while actual markets are becoming less and less perfect and in some areas even disappearing altogether.

My arguments up till now in defense and explanation of the institutional approach in studying economic problems have been developed in terms of logic. And I do believe that we have to continue pressing for logical clarity, at the same time that we in our own work on various problems courageously utilise our broader and theoretically more satisfactory approach.

I foresee that within the next ten or twenty years the now fashionable highly abstract analysis of conventional economists will lose out. Though its logical basis is weak – it is founded on utterly unrealistic, poorly scrutinised, and rarely even explicitly stated assumptions – its decline will be mainly an outcome of the tremendous changes which, with crushing weight, are falling upon us. A more institutional approach will win ground, simply because it is needed to deal in an effective way with the practical and political problems that now tower over us, and which threaten to overwhelm us.

In a sense, the need to study the problems of development in under-developed countries was such a new challenge. The poverty in the backward regions, as they were called, had elicited little interest in the developed countries, and had motivated only slight attention even among economists until the advent of the huge political changes following the Second World War, and in particular the decolonialisation hurricane that swept the globe. When economists then swarmed to study development problems in the new countries, these issues were treated as 'economic' problems in the conventional sense. Economists used concepts and closed models from their work on problems in developed countries, particularly stressing physical investment.

Even when only economic factors were dealt with, the interrelations within a system were not observed. Production in terms of G.N.P. was isolated from distribution, though they are crucially interdependent, particularly in under-developed countries. Economists commonly held consumption outside their growth models, although this is much less warranted in under-developed countries, with their great deprivation in levels of living among the poor masses, which keeps down productivity.

The approach was even narrower than in an earlier generation. Thus as late as the 1950s a group of economists could aspire almost to have made a discovery by stressing the importance of education in development. But they retreated immediately to deal with it as an investment together with physical investment in the capital–output ratio, an approach that Marshall had warned against.

The most serious defect of the closed models utilised when studying the development problems in less-developed countries was that they systematically left out of consideration the non-economic factors. In these countries, which for ages have been socially and economically stagnant, rigid institutions and inflexible attitudes create inhibitions and obstacles to development to a vastly greater extent than those in developed countries.

I cannot in this brief essay further develop my criticism of the inadequacies of studies by conventional economists of the development problems in under-developed countries. In part, the failure of these conventional research efforts can be attributed to the hurried character of their undertaking in the new world political situation after the Second World War. Increasingly, and particularly in recent years, there has, however, been the beginning of a movement toward a more institutional approach that takes into account not only what conventional economists perceive as economic factors, but also institutions and attitudes and the productivity effects of very low levels of living.

This movement has even been reflected in resolutions in various organisations within the United Nations system and in studies and reports by experts called together by them. The demand has been made for a 'unified' or 'integrated' approach to the development problems of less-developed countries. There is an increasing realisation that the models, concepts, and even the whole approach inherent in the conventional economic analysis, lead to gross mistakes. Development must be understood as the movement upward of the entire social system, where there is circular causation between changes of conditions with cumulative effects. Reforms must be directed toward moving the system upward as much and as rapidly as possible by inducing changes planned with this result in mind.

There is still much confusion, much house-cleaning to be undertaken. Many inadequate concepts – for example G.N.P. or unemployment and under-employment – are still carelessly utilised, and many misrepresentative statistics are used which have been collected and analysed in terms of such concepts. But a movement has begun that in the end will give victory to the institutional approach.

Before the oil crisis most of the Western world was already experiencing a persistent – and accelerating – trend toward price inflation. For orderly countries in times of peace this was a new thing. Already then it had here and there tended to pass into 'stagflation' with high or intermittently even rising unemployment while prices were continuing to drift upward. Though generally higher since sometime in the 1950s, interest rates at a time of rapid price increases became very low and often negative in real terms. All countries had learned how to stop a deflation by increasing demand. To stop stagflation turned out to be much more difficult, since the basic causes of the inflationary trend were not on the demand side.

I think it is not an exaggeration to say that our inherited theory had not gone very deeply in clarifying the effects on resource allocation of an inflationary trend, nor even the causes of such a trend. In both respects the analysis would necessitate going much deeper into various institutional conditions that fall outside the closed models and which, therefore, have been largely neglected.

Among those institutional arrangements to begin with are the dynamics of people's expectations, many more peculiarities in the taxation system than are usually observed, and the institutional skewedness of our system of organisations, whereby we all join as income and profit earners but nowhere effectively as consumers. As organisations are represented or have influence in assemblies and governments on all levels, these cannot be relied upon to preserve an economic balance.

The rapid trend in the whole Western world towards consolidation of production, commerce and finance into huge corporations implies the growth of the sectors where prices and wages become administered and are not closely dependent on a market. When at the same time these corporations become multinational and take on the nature of conglomerates, a rapidly growing part of economic and financial transactions escape public awareness and the control of governments. The transactions between governments and defence industries in this era of militarisation of a very large part of our economies can hardly in any country be discussed in simple market terms.

It is in this situation that the oil crisis suddenly broke out, implying a tremendous change in international distribution of incomes and a violent spur of inflation everywhere. And there also developed other scarcities of food and other materials. I cannot in this context attempt to go deeper into accounting for the causes and effects of these towering national and international crises, of which the trend to stagflation is only a limited aspect.

Even if institutional economists as yet have only made sporadic contributions to the analysis of these mounting problems, it is clear that they cannot be analysed in the closed models of inherited economic theory. Much of the present conventional economics will be left at the wayside as irrelevant and uninteresting, while practically and politically interested economists of whatever background will increasingly join the institutional economists. We will be winning not simply because of the logic of our case but because of what is happening in the world. This is partly already happening.

As we tend to become the dominant group, the question can be raised whether we are going to develop the same type of sectarian orthodoxy that has characterised so many economic faculties and journals. I believe not. We will be saved from that by our open models, which do not exclude any fresh orientation in different directions. We will have our differences and the development of economic science will, as usual, proceed through controversies – which is sound. But these controversies will not concern that fundamental methodological principle that what we are studying is not closed beforehand to any causal factor.

6 The Open-System Character of the Economy and its Implications

K. William Kapp

I Introduction

The mainstream of economic theory did not foresee the global environmental crisis just as it did not, in the course of its history, anticipate other important problems which proved to be of major significance. The long-standing neglect of social costs is not the first, and the current food and energy scarcity will not be the last demonstration of the fact that economic theory and practice tend to take account of important problems only under the pressure of public opinion and the urgent necessity of coming to terms with far-reaching negative effects caused by specific emergencies.

Environmental disruption and the growing scarcity of resources have finally made us aware of the fact that production, allocation and the choice of inputs and location are taking place not in closed or semi-closed systems which economic science has traditionally used as theoretical models for the explication of economic processes but in basically open systems. Increasing awareness of the open-system character of production and consumption is, of course, no guarantee that its full methodological and practical consequences are fully comprehended. Have we really understood the full implications of the fact that serious incompatibilities may develop between economic and ecological (as well as social) systems, which threaten the economic process, its social reproduction, and hence the continued guarantee of human well-being and survival?

II Economic Systems as Open Systems

The Physiocrats were the first to perceive the economy as a closed system of interdependent variables. They were led to this realisation partly by the prevailing notions of natural order, the moral philosophy of utilitarianism and the transfer of the equilibrium concept from mechanics to political and economic analysis and partly by their anti-mercantilist policy suggestions which they advanced as practical remedies to cope with the threatening economic and political crisis prior to the French and American Revolutions. The perception of production and reproduction as processes occurring in essentially closed and more or less self-regulatory systems served their pre-analytical notions and supported their normative policy judgements.

Hence the development of closed or semi-closed theoretical models which have survived in the predominant schools of economics both in its neoclassical and its Keynesian versions and have continued to shape the scope of conventional analysis, the formulation of basic concepts and, last but not least, the delimitation of the scope of its subject-matter. Institutional and, to a lesser extent, Marxist economists have always criticised this narrow scope of conventional economic theory and have insisted that economic systems are parts of a much broader political and institutional system from which they receive important impulses and which they, in turn, are capable of influencing and even changing in a variety of ways.

The degradation of the physical and social environment and the exhaustion of important non-renewable (capital) resources have merely added a new and decisive illustration of the fact that economic systems are intimately and reciprocally related to other systems and are in this sense fundamentally open systems. To view the economy as a closed system may be methodologically convenient and enable economic theory to formulate its concepts and theories in accordance with the canons of formal mathematical logic, but this tends to perpetuate a wrong perception of reality which narrows our theoretical horizon. In fact, the resulting perspective and the criteria of evaluation are those in terms of which the system of business enterprise tends to evaluate its performance. While this may be an explanation it is no justification for the continued adherence to the traditional closed-system approach of economic science which, as an empirical system of knowledge, must follow the lead of its subject-matter if its conclusions are not to become misleading and irrelevant.

The current discussion of environmental disruption has used air and water pollution caused by the emission of waste residuals by producers and consumers as typical illustrations of the impact of production and consumption on the environment. We are far from denying the importance and the typical character of the social costs represented by air and water pollution. In fact, they are the classical cases which have led to the growing awareness of the interdependence of economic and ecological systems. However, we have chosen modern agriculture in order to illustrate the essentially global and open-system character of economic processes and to show the full range of global consequences which production and specific techniques, that is economic choices guided by market costs and returns, may have upon ecological balance, society and social reproduction.

III Modern Agriculture as an Illustration of the Global and Open-System Character of the Economy

Agriculture, both in developed and less-developed countries, employs new techniques and new capital inputs with far-reaching ecological and socio-economic consequences. In fact, modern farming has become a highly capital-intensive mechanised industrial activity. High-yielding varieties have changed the character of agricultural production. The increased yields of these new varieties are due to their specific effective and 'aggressive' feeding characteristics which speed up the depletion of the soil. This, in turn, requires the application of considerable amounts of chemical fertilisers in addition to other complementary inputs as, for instance, water and pesticides as well as additional capital inputs such as farm machinery, tractors, harvesters, spraying equipment, aeroplanes, and so forth. It is these inputs that account for the higher yield per acre or per farm worker. As a result of these technological changes fields have become larger and the average size of farm has increased; plowing, sowing, the application of fertilisers, spraying of insecticides, harvesting, poultry raising, cattle breeding, feeding, milking, and so on – all have become mechanised operations resembling the assembly line in other industries. Millions of farms have disappeared; the rural population has declined and moved to cities thus adding to urban congestion and overcrowding.

The ecological consequences of these technical and structural changes may be summarised briefly and succinctly. Technology and mechanisation have taken command by imposing their imperatives upon farming as an industry. What used to be a highly diversified (biological) system of growing food and primary materials has been transformed into large-scale and highly specialised monocultures. Moreover, modern farming has become a major user of capital goods produced by farm-supporting industries employing an increasing number of industrial labourers and making heavy and increasing demands on scarce resources, particularly electricity and petroleum. Thus agriculture is now a major consumer of scarce energy and, viewed as a whole, uses perhaps more petroleum than any other single industry. In fact, farming has become a way of turning petroleum into food. Our harvests of food and primary materials may indeed be said to be 'harvests of oil'.[1] Despite the fact that farming could be a net energy-producing sector of the economy – by capturing the energy of the sun – and despite the growing energy crisis, we continue to measure efficiency in farming in terms of output per hour of labour or per acre instead of measuring it, for example, in terms of output per unit of energy.[2] This dependence of modern agriculture on petroleum is particularly dangerous for those countries which, like India, have opted for a 'Green Revolution' and the use of high-yielding varieties, and are now experiencing the first signs of a stagnation of their output.[3]

Nor is this all; the application of chemical fertilisers and the utilisation of pesticides (insecticides, herbicides, fungicides) are subject to diminishing returns. Hence, increasing doses of chemicals need to be applied to secure additional returns per unit of input. Not all of these chemicals can be assimilated by plants; they find their way into rivers and lakes. Growing specialisation with its emphasis on monocultures has made crops more susceptible to sudden massive losses due to pest invasions. The new varieties are themselves less resistant than non-hybrid varieties. Moreover, pesticides may kill not only the pests but their enemies as well; in addition, the resistance and immunity of certain pests are known to increase by natural selection. Hence increasing doses of pesticides are necessary in order to compensate for the loss of their effectiveness. Furthermore, modern farming tends to use pesticides quite mechanically according to generalised spraying time schedules provided by the manufacturers. This has led to indiscriminate operations of 'over-kill' which continue as long as additional applications of pesticides are, or are believed to be, profitable; in other words, returns are calculated without considering the system-wide social losses or the inflated price rises and other 'imperfections' of the market for farm products. It is true, costs may also be inflated due to 'administered' and inflated oligopolistic prices of farm inputs but the fact remains that the guiding commercial cost–benefit calculations according to which pesticides (and fertilisers) are being applied, do not take into account their ecologically negative consequences.[4] The neglect of the social costs resulting from ecological hazards to flora, fauna and human beings, as well as the substantial energy requirements for the production of chemical inputs, is only one aspect of the situation; the other is the failure to take account of potential benefits of alternative techniques of production.

Finally, the new crops seem to be characterised by relatively low protein contents, that is a lower capacity (for example of hybrid corn) to feed and raise animals. This, in turn, has called for more imports of fish protein in the form of fish meal to supplement animal diets. As a result of these undoubtedly profitable imports – profitable both for the Peruvian fishing and export industries and the U.S. and European importers of protein-rich fish meal – we are confronted with the ecologically and, if properly calculated, also economically absurd situation that a continent with protein-poor diets (South America) supports today the relatively protein-rich diets of highly developed countries.[5] Monetary or market criteria of efficiency and of economic rationality and the resulting export–import pattern tend to give rise to a global allocation of inputs and a distribution of outputs which may be far from desirable either ecologically or in the light of a concept of substantive rationality which would take account of actual human requirements in different parts of the world. (We are not suggesting that Peru should stop all exports of fish protein to countries with protein-rich diets and should instead cover the protein deficiencies of South America. Export of fish meal will have to remain an important source of foreign exchange to pay for Peru's imports of capital goods. However, the existence of this protein-rich supply of fish and the widespread deficiency of the diet of Peru's poor population, as indeed of the population of the rest of South America, provides at least a basis for a realistic search for alternative solutions and new patterns of foreign trade. The problem under discussion is the neglect of basic nutritional needs in the process of planning and development.)

As a preliminary conclusion we may say that the organising principles of economic systems guided by exchange values are incompatible with the requirements of ecological systems and the satisfaction of basic human needs. Our traditional criteria of technical efficiency, of cost–benefit calculations and of economic rationality are the crucial points under discussion. Their limitations become manifest as soon as we view the dynamic interaction of open social and economic systems with specific ecological systems.

It is hardly necessary to add that, if we accept this point of view, as we believe we must, new criteria of rational action and planning are called for. Above all, alternative solutions different from those which we have pursued in the light of the narrow economic calculus in terms of market criteria impose themselves. In the concrete case of modern agriculture it may perhaps be useful to be more explicit in order to counteract any possible misinterpretation of our position. We are not suggesting a return to traditional agriculture or a ban on fertilisers, pesticides and modern technology; rather, the practical and theoretical implications of our position are to abandon our traditional notions of efficiency and rationality and to redefine them in the light of the 'new' realities of the interdependency of systems. In view of the system-wide repercussions of agricultural production, and indeed of production in general, it must be clear that neither technical feasibility nor technological imperatives nor micro-economic rationality, in terms of net private returns and entrepreneurial costs can provide adequate answers to the question of what are desirable aims and policies. Criteria of economic performance can neither be derived from technical feasibility nor from economic efficiency in the narrow sense, but must be formulated in the light of a system-wide appraisal of ecological, social and economic advantages and disadvantages. As far as modern agriculture and the need for high levels of output and productivity are concerned, it will be necessary to envisage and appraise a whole bundle of complementary aims and alternative strategies, such as a greater diversification of crops, the planting of specific crops in geographic regions less affected by pests, a return to appropriate crop rotation, the development of pest resistant varieties which have the desirable yield and quality characteristics, the systematic implementation of bio-environmental controls,[6] and greater reliance on monitoring pest populations with a shift from methods of 'over-kill' or even '100 per cent pest elimination' to 'treatment when necessary' and the application of pesticides as stop-gap emergency measures. In countries like the United States, the return to cultivation of some of the nearly 60 million acres taken out of production at a cost of three to four billion dollars annually could compensate for the possible increase of crop losses due to a reduction of the present over-intensive application of pesticides with its disruptive effects on the environment.[7]

IV The Open-System Approach

Of course, it is insufficient to say that the use of destructive technologies and techniques applied in accordance with the principle of maximising net returns has 'external' effects on regional, national and international scales. Nor will it be sufficient to call for more information and more interdisciplinary research. All this is true enough. As our discussion of modern agriculture has shown, the appropriate unit of analysis is neither the individual farm, nor the national farm economy, nor a particular ecological system. The relevant unit of analysis is much larger and the time span that counts is much longer than those in terms of which business enterprise and economic science have traditionally perceived and defined the notions of efficiency, rationality and optimality.

Thus the environmental crisis forces economists to acknowledge the limitations of their methodological and cognitive approaches and to reconsider the scope of their science. The classical economists – Adam Smith and his successors – could still claim with some justification that economic systems could be understood as semi-closed systems because, in their time, air, water, and so forth were, in a sense, 'free' goods and because they were convinced – wrongly – that rational action – under competitive conditions – had only positive social effects. This belief has turned out to be an illusion. To hold on to it in the face of the environmental crisis can only be regarded as a self-deception and a deception to others. Contemporary economists who continue to discuss economic and environmental problems in closed systems have much less of an excuse for this practice than the classical economists. Human action and economic decisions relating to production are not taking place in closed or even semi-closed systems but within a network of relationships and dynamic structures in continuous open interaction with one another. In short, we need a new approach which makes it possible to deal with the dynamic interrelations between economic systems and the whole network of physical and social systems and, indeed, the entire composite system of structural relationships. It would be an illusion to believe that such a system view of the economy can or will emerge from the traditional modes of analytical thinking; nor would it be realistic to expect systems thinking 'to spring into existence in a mature state. . .it must evolve out of proposals, discussions, reformulations and experience'.[8] Systems thinking is inevitably complex inasmuch as it is concerned with discontinuous non-linear 'feedback' effects which characterise the dynamic interdependencies between the different systems as well as of each subsystem with the composite whole. In this sense, it is indeed a 'step away from traditional science'.[9] It is, by its very nature, multi-dimensional, multi-disciplinary and integrative. Thinking in terms of interdependent systems is an innovation and presupposes a new outlook which calls for an abandonment of old knowledge 'before the new can be created'.[10] Such innovation is, as a rule, experienced as a source of annoyance, a destroyer of routine, an underminer of complacency.[11] Innovations of this kind can hardly be expected to come from scholars with a conventional outlook but call for a wider range of reference than the representatives of 'normal' science bring to bear upon their subject-matter.[12]

While ecologists and natural scientists, as a rule, have a better understanding of complex interdependencies they too will have to widen their perspective in dealing with environmental and other global problems. Few ecologists seem to have dealt with the impact of economic decision-making and technological factors upon ecological systems; nor have they sufficiently come to terms with human values and problems of costs. 'Ecology works very well for families of plants and groups of animals, but up to now there does not exist an individual human ecology.'[13] We are only at the beginning of thinking in terms of interdependent systems and considerable research will be required to close the gaps in our knowledge as to the structure and interaction of a multitude of systems and their 'performance'. Nevertheless, it would be a mistake to believe that we have to start from zero. Systems analysis has a long history in other disciplines such as biology, particularly micro-biology, genetics, chemistry, nuclear physics and, last but not least, cultural anthropology.[14]

Of course, it will not suffice to aim at a merely formal representation of the open-system character of the economy in its interaction with something called environment. What is required is to overcome the essentially dualistic conceptualisation of economy and environment in order to give our analysis the necessary empirical content. Determination of basic needs and requirements of health and survival, of environmental norms and maximum tolerable levels of contamination; environmental-impact studies of alternative technologies in specific localities rather than linear physical flow models are some of the empirical and quantitative problems that call for exploration and analysis; social science will have to come to terms with the key problem of the open-system character of the economy – the fact, namely, that production derives material inputs from the physical and decisive impulses from the social system which, in turn, may be disrupted and disorganised by the emission of residual wastes up to a point where social reproduction itself may be threatened.

Systems thinking will have to avoid a number of pitfalls, some of which may be listed briefly within the context of the present discussion: the tendency of concentrating attention on aggregates and their historical correlation without a causal analysis of the effects of specific technologies, production, consumption and income patterns; the use of constant coefficients of correlation and the neglect of circular cumulative interdependencies; the failure to consider the influence of institutional factors including the role of vested and conflicting interest groups; the insistence upon determinate and precise solutions of formal problems instead of a search for practical and useful answers to urgent practical problems; and the neglect of a careful appraisal of alternative goals and technologies as well as of their opportunity costs and potential social impacts.

V Economics as a Normative Science

The methodological and cognitive implications of the fact that economic systems are not closed but are fundamentally open systems would be far-reaching. Above all, it would be necessary to take account of the complex interaction and circular interdependencies between different systems. Production and consumption put in motion complex processes which have serious and determinable negative consequences on the physical and social environment with an inevitable impact on distribution;

these interdependencies imply a forced transfer of 'unpaid' social costs, which constitute a secondary redistribution of real income primarily (but not exclusively) to economically weaker members of society as well as to future generations. Moreover, individuals and groups whose income and health are adversely affected by destructive technologies under specific institutional arrangements are victims of a process of production over which they have no control, and against which they have no adequate legal redress. These inter-system relations with redistributive effects are not exchange or market relations. They represent extra-market physical flows from corporate production units and individual households to the environment and back from the latter to the former. The character of these flows needs to be understood and subjected to empirical and theoretical analysis and appraisal.[15] These non-market physical flows raise important problems of circular cumulative causation which must be recognised as typical characteristics of economic processes.[16] They have a direct bearing on actual costs and benefits; they are neither 'external' nor are they voluntary or contractual. In short, they are extra-market phenomena and market prices do not provide adequate (if indeed any) criteria for their evaluation.

The actual costs may be regional or system-wide in character because pollution affects not only single individuals in specific localities but entire groups of people and regions, extending frequently beyond national boundaries. Its effects, moreover, will be unequally distributed. The same applies to practically all other negative effects of environmental degradation. Noise, urban and traffic congestion, industrial accidents, occupational and civilisational diseases, fatigue, frustration – are only some of the symptoms of serious social dislocation experienced by individuals but system-wide in their repercussions and significance. Their impact will be felt in the form of a deterioration and dehumanisation of the quality of the living and working conditions of millions of people both today and in the future. These phenomena raise complex problems of measuring and evaluating environmental costs (and benefits) which are not solved by such conceptual tools as revealed preferences, willingness to pay or to compensate, Pareto optimality and so on, for these concepts are derived from our traditional approach based upon a 'methodological subjectivism'. The validity of this has never been generally accepted even in those fields of analysis for which they were originally developed. Instead of attempting to calculate benefit and cost in terms of subjective preferences and exchange values it would be necessary to assess the environmental and social impact of these physical flows socially and hence politically and to translate 'physical and social impacts into politically understandable and relevant trade-offs'.[17] Only in this way can we hope to arrive at reasoned choices between conflicting interests and objectives in the light of explicit political and, hence, moral judgements rather than in terms of calculated 'shadow' prices and costs derived from market values, which, upon closer analysis, can be shown to reflect either the subjective preferences and valuations of the experts and/or of powerful vested interests.[18]

The degradation of the physical and social environment and the recognition of economic systems as open systems would make it necessary to define socially desirable macroeconomic goals (or norms) of the economy. These social goals include a number of conflicting general objectives such as greater equality or justice in distribution, economic stability, full employment, efficiency in the utilisation of scarce resources, participation in decision-making, and so forth. At the same time, they will have to include the maintenance of dynamic states of ecological and economic balance as one of the fundamental prerequisites of socio-economic reproduction and growth. The definition and concrete determination of such macroeconomic goals is not an easy matter partly because they require a considerable amount of knowledge regarding the effects of alternative levels of output on the environment; of the consequences of alternative inputs, technologies and locations which, in the light of the carrying capacity of the environment, can be tolerated.

The determination of such macroeconomic goals requires an interdisciplinary-research effort which exceeds the competence of economists but which cannot be conducted without them. However, we do not believe that the price mechanism and the monetary calculus can be relied upon for the evaluation and determination of the relative importance of different goods and services including the choice of inputs, techniques and location, and this for several reasons. In the first place, the price mechanism and an evaluation in monetary terms reflect the willingness to pay of individuals and groups and hence also the inequality in the distribution of income and market power. The supply and demand mechanism is, in this sense, essentially a non-egalitarian and elitist mechanism of evaluating goods, services and environmental damages. Furthermore, the market and monetary calculus is not adapted to the social evaluation either of environmental damages or the type of public goods and services required for the maintenance of dynamic states of ecological and economic balance. We are not arguing that it is impossible to place a monetary value upon environmental damages or for that matter on the public goods and services. After all it is always possible to evaluate them at their monetary costs. However, it can be shown that monetary evaluation, in this sense, fails to ascertain and express their relative social importance in the sense of value to society (and individuals) both in the short and in the long run. Human life and human health may be evaluated in monetary terms (for example in terms of the accumulated income earned or lost over time at compound interest), but is such a procedure cognitively warranted? For several reasons we hold that such a procedure is not justifiable because monetary values are not an adequate criteria in terms of which the qualities under consideration can be expressed and measured.[19]

The fact that we deal with collective (public) goods and services and with dynamic states of balance including the use and exhaustion of non-renewable (capital) resources which will have negative effects on future generations complicates matters and make all monetary evaluations problematical if not indeed unacceptable and cognitively irrelevant. In short, as soon as the open character of economic systems is fully realised the formulation of social goals and objectives and the problem of collective choices can no longer be avoided. Such objectives and choices with respect to the maintenance of dynamic states of ecological and economic balance essential for the maintenance and improvement of the conditions of social and individual existence (quality of life) must become the point of departure for a normative science of economics. The elaboration of a quantitative framework for these social objectives is currently under way in the form of the development of work on social and environmental indicators. Such indicators provide at least the first step and the basis upon which social and environmental normative judgements and collective (political) decisions and priorities could be formulated. Here is the open frontier and the unexplored territory for normative economics.[20]

The next step would be the elaboration of the necessary strategies or alternative courses of action designed to guarantee the attainment of social goals decided upon. This is essentially a task of choosing alternative instruments of control (and economic policies) with a view to assuring that the desired social goals are indeed reached. These measures of control will have to go beyond the scope of traditional economic policies, for they will be concerned with the assessment and choice of technologies, of the quality and quantity of specific inputs and location, and with the change of behavioural and motivational patterns of producers and consumers. An equally if not more important task would be the systematic search for new inputs, alternative technologies, new patterns of location as well as new patterns of consumption or styles of life. In other words, the fact that economic systems are not closed but open systems which depend for their reproduction upon inputs drawn from the physical environment into which they emit pollutants and destructive residuals makes it necessary to consider most of the factors which economic theory has so far regarded as constant or given data as the very problem which needs to be solved or, methodologically speaking, as dependent variables. They are neither constant nor given. The socially warranted technologies, the required inputs (including the location of production) are not known beforehand; on the contrary, they need to be explored and determined. Which technologies, which input pattern, which locations are to be chosen and, ultimately, which output and which institutional behaviour patterns are required and socially warranted are in fact the very problems which call for a solution and which a normative science of economics would have to elucidate and help to explore in the light of the desirable social goals and objectives and the system-wide consequences and actual costs of alternative courses of action. In short, a normative science of economics taking account of the open-system character of the economy would imply a complete reversal of the analytical procedures of the discipline as hitherto practised and applied. Instead of postulating a given state of technology, given behaviour patterns and given individual preferences and aiming at the explication of the allocation mechanism of a hypothetically closed system under autonomous and self-regulating market forces and on the assumption of rational optimising action of individual producers and consumers, the new task of economics would be to elucidate the manner in which collectively determined social goals and objectives could be attained in the most effective and socially least-costly manner.[21]

Two final observations may be useful with respect to both the concept of economic efficiency and also the educational requirements which the open system and normative approach to economics calls for. If economic systems are fundamentally open systems, and if, as we have implied throughout our discussion, uncontrolled economic decisions based upon the calculation of entrepreneurial costs and returns are basically incompatible with the maintenance of dynamic states of ecological and economic balance,[22] not only the concepts of costs and returns but, above all, those of economic efficiency and optimality need to be redefined and reformulated. They have to be broadened to take account of the fact that what may be efficient and optimal in a closed system of production and distribution may be inefficient and anything but optimal in the long run and may be destructive from a social and global viewpoint due to the neglected cumulative effect of the inter-system interactions between open systems.

The educational implications of the open-system character of the economy are equally far-reaching. Instead of introducing students in economics, especially freshmen, to the highly esoteric formal apparatus which fills the conventional textbooks it seems to me indispensible that they must first be introduced to the open character of economic systems. Systems thinking while undoubtedly complex offers no unsurmountable difficulties for the beginner. Problems of entropy (that is the tendency of increasing disorganisation), of feedback effects (that is the fact that part of the output is fed back and affects succeeding inputs and outputs), material balances, maximum limits of contamination, cumulative causation, need to become part of the teaching of economics in order to prepare economists of the future for the tasks with which they will be increasingly concerned.

VI 'Conceptual Freeze' or Intellectual Reconstruction

It was not our purpose to predict the future of economics but to show a possible and, in our estimation, necessary direction of its change and reconstruction. Of course, having come this far we face the question as to whether the notion of a normative science of economics is not a vision of an alternative which has no possibility of being realised in the calculable future. Is it not more likely that economists will continue to view economic systems as essentially closed systems and to hold on to the established procedures and methods? There is indeed considerable evidence for an affirmative answer to this question. Neoclassical economic theory, just as the market economy, have shown a remarkable capacity to assimilate new problems and new developments. In this context we are thinking, for example, of such proposals as the establishment of private or public property rights with respect to rivers and lakes or the suggestion that rights to pollute (pollution permits) be sold and bought at auctions and/or be made the subject of bilateral negotiations between polluters and those who are damaged by pollution. What these proposals amount to is, in fact, a return to the conventional wisdom of relying on property rights and market costs and returns instead of preserving the principle of maintaining communal rights to nature and treating them as social use-values serving fundamental human requirements. We are also thinking of the current tendency of assimilating social costs into conventional economics by means of the empty-box concept of 'externalities' or of proposals for the 'internalisation' of social costs through fiscal policies, subsidies, and so on. I feel that neither the concept of externalities nor the introduction of social-cost curves into formal theory nor current proposals of 'deducting' social costs from gross or net national product measurements will get us very far. For these attempts to incorporate new facts 'painlessly' into conventional theory[23] follow the classical pattern which Veblen once described as the typical response of traditional economics to new 'facts'. In an age of business enterprise, Veblen wrote, new facts and ideas will impose themselves upon the imagination of a wider audience of economists and practical men of affairs only if they are expressed in terms of business finance and the market test. Veblen felt that ingrained habits of thought, reflecting the predominant climate of opinion characteristic of a system of business enterprise, had a tendency of being transmitted from one generation of economists to the next as they were prone to do in the past, that is via 'institutions of higher learning'. For this reason, Veblen, in his time, regarded the prospects for a reconstruction of economics as dim.[24] Of course, Veblen knew what he was talking about; he knew from his own experience as an analyst and as a critic of the system of business enterprise that established theories resist any change and do not simply fade away because they are in conflict with empirical evidence.

However, since Veblen published his essay on economics in 'the calculable future' some fifty years ago, economic conditions have changed and the gap between theory and reality has widened. The deterioration of the environment constitutes a more fundamental challenge to the scope and method of traditional economics than anything that has happened before. In addition, practically all the great current problems (such as inflation, the increase of oil prices, unemployment, monetary disequilibria and balance-of-payments deficits, the population explosion and the scarcity of food as well as famines) are not only world-wide phenomena but call for new global approaches and solutions.

Moreover, these problems call for the formulation of specific goals and objectives and the selection and mobilisation of the necessary means (technologies, inputs, controls). It is true, unemployment may be 'remedied' by military and other expenditures even though the current inability to curb the inflationary impact of continuous public domestic and international deficits and the creation of new international 'liquidities' including the recycling of petro-dollars still present open and unsolved if not unsolvable problems within the framework of a 'market economy'. While unemployment may be reduced by an expansion of production, the degradation of the environment will increase with greater output unless alternative criteria of determining inputs and outputs as well as the choice of technology and of location are developed. For these reasons, the need for a reconstruction of economics under the impact of the current global crisis will increase and so will the pressure for a theoretical and methodological innovation of contemporary theories. While it is possible that the desire to retain the traditional doctrine may make the latter more and more dogmatic and give rise to a 'conceptual freeze',[25] it is not unlikely that this freeze will be broken in the calculable future under the impact of new facts, new evidence of environmental disruption, new catastrophes and an increasing public opposition to the deterioration of the physical and social environment.

7 Towards a New Political Economy

Shigeto Tsuru

It is symptomatic of the wind of change in economic thinking that the standard textbook of economics by Paul A. Samuelson finally conceded in its ninth edition (1973) that 'the theory of distribution is still in an unsettled state',[1] and also reworded the phrase in the eighth edition which read: 'Adam Smith's Invisible Hand, which tried to convert mankind's selfish interest to a best solution of society's *what, how*, and *for whom* problems', into a new one in the ninth which now reads: 'Adam Smith's Invisible Hand, which tried to convert mankind's selfish interest to a best solution of society's *what* and *how* problems (but, alas, not necessarily to a best solution of the *for whom* problems).'[2]

Here scepticism is cast on the distributional adequacy of the competitive market mechanism. But the fact of 'market failure' in all its aspects is now so widely accepted that it may not be necessary to explicate on them. Competitive market mechanism, if it is to succeed in 'converting mankind's selfish interest to a best solution of society's *what, how* and *for whom* problems' and thus to have a normative significance in itself, requires that (1) barometric indicators such as prices, wage rates, interest rates, and so forth should reflect changes in economic data faithfully and are not to be tampered with; (2) consumer sovereignty, with all its implications, should reign; and (3) external effects, either favourable or negative, are, for all practical purposes, negligible.

In present-day capitalist societies none of these conditions is now satisfactorily met.

As to the first requirement above, the practice of administered prices is rampant today in numerous industries, and the mark-up pricing which exists subsumes that amount of profit which a firm intends to make use of for the purpose of its own expansion either in plant and equipment or in external investment. The rigidity of wage and interest rates is well-known. And even some neoclassical economists, including Paul Samuelson, have lately begun to speak of 'powers' as an effective concept in the analysis of market equilibrium. Needless to say, the fact that market barometers in fact are not working as expected does not mean that the parametric function of prices cannot be made to work. The price system *could* be made, as Lange suggested,[3] more comprehensive in a planned economy than under capitalism and utilised as a tool of planning for efficient resource allocation, while divorcing it from direct distributional implications.

The demise of consumer sovereignty is now an old story. One of the basic premises for this concept is that each individual consumer knows, through his own judgement, what is best for him, and acts accordingly. The content of this premise, however, is not at all unambiguous. Any act by any consumer can be said to satisfy this condition if we emulate Abraham Lincoln, who, when asked how tall a man's legs should be, replied, 'Tall enough to reach the ground.' This is a tautological requirement which everyone's legs can satisfy. And yet some libertarian economists often assert that it is better that a man act unwisely of his own free will – provided, always, his action harms no other persons – than that he be coerced into a wiser course of action.

As a matter of fact, it is not easy, nor costless, to ascertain what is best for oneself. If one is in the state of subsistence living, one knows, without being told by anyone, what is needed to sustain oneself. Basic needs for food, clothing and shelter are the items of consumption which, when lacking, will be recognised even by a six-year old. But once we come to the sphere of discretionary consumption items, which of course proliferate as living standards rise, consumers cannot but escape from what Galbraith called the 'dependence effect'. All the knowledge and wherewithal to persuade the consumers to purchase a certain item are on the side of suppliers and it is practically impossible, even for a co-operative body of consumers, to match this expertise. In fact, more and more of the items of discretionary consumption are becoming highly sophisticated in technical details, and very often the suppliers do not reveal even what they themselves know to be the deficiencies of the product or its likely effect on the user's health.

More important, the alternatives offered to consumers are confined to what suppliers choose to make available; and it happens quite often that consumers have no way of registering in the market their genuine demand for a certain good even when that good is for the satisfaction of a basic need. Observe, for example, the gradual disappearance of public baths in Japanese cities in the circumstance where many of the city dwellers are not equipped with private bathrooms in their homes. Again, one may be free to choose among a dozen models of automobiles; but one who has been accustomed, and still desires, to commute by a bus would not be able to register his choice as a consumer once the bus line is abolished (because of declining business and congestion of the road).

As for the third of the requirements, namely that external effects, either favourable or negative, are for all practical purposes negligible, most of us have become lately aware that the dimension of the problem is now of a different order compared with the days of Alfred Marshall and that spillover effects of various kinds can hardly be said to be 'negligible'. The United Nations Conference on Human Environment held in Stockholm (1972) impressed upon us all that the rapid economic growth accompanied by high-level technological development in advanced countries has created in its train a host of intractable external diseconomies such as organic mercury poisoning, cadmium poisoning, photo-chemical smog, and so on which certainly should constitute negative items in the calculation of net economic welfare. Some of these externalities could be internalised, either as *ex post* or *ex ante* cost, within the atomistic accounting of their originating industries or individuals. The 'polluter pay' principle, proposed as a guideline by the O.E.C.D., is an example of such a device. But just as a public good, by its very nature, is characterised by a joint-consumption possibility ('the more for you there is, the more for me!') and non-excludability ('we cannot exclude the non-payer from making use of it!'), both of which characteristics are the antithesis of market principles, modern environmental spillovers partake very often of a character of 'negative public good' which, too, defies market simulation. We may agree that *ex ante* internalisation is always preferrable to *ex post* internalisation, but not only is the former unavoidably subject to a wide range of predictive judgements as to consequences but also it is often the case that, even with the best of calculations, a grave risk may have to be taken. The development of nuclear fission energy is a case in point. The problem here is wrought with so many unascertainable risks that the usual cost–benefit analysis is unable to cope with the dimension involved. Allen Kneese wrote that

> It is my belief that benefit–cost analysis cannot answer the most important policy question associated with the desirability of developing a large-scale, fission-based economy. To expect it to do so is to ask it to bear a burden it cannot sustain. This is so because these questions have to do with whether society should strike the Faustian bargain with atomic scientists and engineers .... If so unforgiving a technology as large-scale nuclear fission energy production is adopted, it will impose a burden of continuous monitoring and sophisticated management of a dangerous material, essentially forever. The penalty of not bearing this burden may be unparalleled disaster.[4]

In other words, we have come, in the advance of our technology and productive powers, to a stage where external effects of a negative character could transcend the type of economic calculation which simulates the market transaction accounting.

The celebrated phrase by Adam Smith referring to an 'invisible hand' has guided economists for almost two centuries. Thus,

> Every individual endeavors to employ his capital so that its produce may be of greatest value .... He generally neither intends to promote the public interest, nor knows how much he is promoting it. He intends only his own security ... only his own gain. And he is in this led by an Invisible Hand to promote an end which was no part of his intention. ...By pursuing his own interest he frequently promotes that of society more effectually than when he really intends to promote it.[5]

Here it is implied that the competitive market mechanism, if left alone, achieves its own *normative* significance and that what economists should do is to let the market have its full sway foreclosing any artificial interference with it. In a sense, this task is a simple one since it does not involve detailing of any concrete recommendations beyond saying '*laissez-faire, laissez-passez*!' Leaving things alone could be a policy of normative character in itself.

Once, however, the failure of the market is admitted, the picture is entirely different. For it means that the 'invisible hand' does not work and that 'someone' has to take into his own hands the task of guiding the economy towards certain specific normative goals. It would not be sufficient to say, 'Interfere somehow!' This 'somehow' has to be specified with regard to the method *and* the target. In other words, *economics* has to become *political economy* again with its normative aspects concretely specified and the strategies spelled out.

In fact, there is a more far-reaching implication in this evolution of the discipline. Earlier we referred to the fact of various 'barometers' of the market mechanism becoming rigid and contrived. Some of our colleagues still feel apparently that flexibility can, and should, be restored to these 'barometers'. Here lies, however, a basic question of whether it can be done. It was Karl Marx himself who prophetically wrote more than a century ago that

> As large-scale industry advances, the creation of real wealth depends less on the labour time and the quantity of labour expended than on the power of instrumentalities set in motion during the labour time. These instrumentalities, and their powerful effectiveness, are in no proportion to the immediate labour time which their production requires; their effectiveness rather depends on the attained level of science and technological progress; in other words, on the application of this science to production. . . .In this transformation, the great pillar of production and wealth is no longer the immediate labour performed by man himself, nor his labour time, but the appropriation of his own universal productivity, i.e., his knowledge and his mastery of nature through his societal existence – in one word: the development of the societal individual. . . .As soon as human labour, in its immediate form, has ceased to be the great source of wealth, labour time will cease, and must of necessity cease to be the measure of wealth, and the exchange value must of necessity cease to be the measure of use value. . . .The mode of production which rests on the exchange value thus collapses.[6]

In Marx's mind was a thesis that the development of productive forces inevitably conditions the transformation of the mode of production; and it was his view that the conditions for the atomistic attribution of labour's contribution to final products would inevitably disappear as automation and other forms of application of science to production progressed, and the 'societal individual' came to be developed. If the mode of production which rests on the exchange value thus comes to be undermined, it will be only natural that the determination of factor prices (the wage rate and the rate of interest) will lose the market objectivity of impersonal character and will become the product of power relations.

We may be already in such a stage in the evolving mode of production so that private firms (at least in the 'planning system' in the Galbraithian sense) can more or less determine the size of their mark-up ratio, and the organised workers can successfully obtain their scheduled wage demands from their employers.[7] To the extent factor prices are *administered* in such a way instead of being objectively determined in competitive markets, then what is expected of the 'invisible hand' is further undermined. Not only is it the case that the market no longer serves as an impersonal arena through which consumers' sovereign decisions are faithfully conveyed to suppliers, but it must further be admitted that factor markets do not perform the function expected of them of objectively determining the rates at which factors are rewarded in proportion to their contributions to the total product. In fact, we may have come to a stage in our technical progress where it is becoming increasingly difficult to relate marginal input of a factor to incremental output. In addition, we observe in present-day capitalist societies an undeniable tendency of large units of private capital to embrace the market itself within their planning system, thus taking the role of the 'invisible hand' into their own hands. As Galbraith has written,

> If . . . with the rise of the great corporation goes the power extensively to enforce its will on the society – not only to fix prices and costs but to influence consumers, and organize the supply of materials and components, and mobilize its own savings and capital, and develop a strategy for handling labour, and influence the attitudes of the community and the actions of the state – then the purposes of its controlling intelligence, of its technostructure, become of the highest importance. They are not confined by the market. They transcend the market, use the market as an instrument and are the chariot to which society, if not chained, is at least attached.[8]

Such is the background against which we have to grope our way seeking positive directions for a 'new' political economy in the coming future.

Once we depart from reliance on competitive market equilibrium, which in itself had normative implications, economists are called upon to extend their enquiry in two directions: (1) to be prepared to make normative judgements; and (2) to widen the scope of enquiry to encompass what were once regarded as externalities. The former task requires specifying the processes through which a normative judgement can be derived from social consensus, and the latter task implies replacing the idea of economics as being a closed equilibrium system with that of it being an open-ended discipline having symbiotic contact with neighbouring disciplines. Frank Knight could say over fifty years ago, writing on the system of free enterprise,

> That free enterprise is not a perfectly ideal system of social organization is a proposition not to be gainsaid ... [But] its weaknesses and failures ... lie outside the field of the mechanics of exchange under the theoretical conditions of perfect competition ... [and] the values of life are not, in the main, reducible to satisfactions obtained from the consumption of exchangeable goods and services ... [for] desires [are] the product of social influence ... [and] productive capacities ... are derived from an uncertain mixture of conscientious effort, inheritance, pure luck and outright force and fraud.[9]

But it is clear today that economics as a social science cannot content itself by smugly, or nonchalantly, repeating the dictum that 'the values of life are not, in the main, reducible to satisfactions obtained from the consumption of exchangeable goods and services'.

If normative enquiry is inescapable in the discipline, where should we begin? Probably the most significant from the social point of view would be the problem of fair distribution both within a single economy and across the rich and poor nations in the world. We have seen earlier that even within a limited theoretical framework of neoclassical economics itself the unquestioned authority, Samuelson, came to admit that 'the theory of distribution is still in an unsettled state'. In a broader vista encompassing social *desiderata* on which an increasing consensus is being gained, we recognise that the distribution problem constitutes a challenge today less in the sense of needing a theoretical explanation than in the sense of needing a positive solution in practice. If one takes the view, as the present author does, that the neoclassical theory of distribution is bankrupt and is unable to cope with the changing mode of production as conditioned by modern technical progress, one's approach to the task of practical solution in this sphere can be *direct*, bypassing the paraphernalia of marginalism. One can begin by specifying a basket of 'civil minima' in the category of basic consumption goods and services. Contents of such a basket may, of course, differ for each country. But the international 'civil minima' may also be specified. Then next comes the question of how to ensure the basket for each citizen. Here a variety of measures are available. Many societies already provide certain basic needs without *quid pro quo* or have the experience of having done so in time of war. Broadly speaking, two approaches exist: (1) the income-guarantee approach and (2) the provision-in-kind approach. In both cases, fiscal redistribution is needed, and here again there could be a variety of tax measures available, from progressive and negative income taxes to the transaction taxes of socialist countries. In this connection it may be relevant to point out here that, in face of the persisting inflationary trend in most of the advanced capitalist countries, the social *desiderata* of guaranteeing a basket of 'civil minima' would be easier to achieve by the provision-in-kind approach although the administrative cost is likely to be higher in this case than in the income guarantee approach.

Reorientation of economics towards normative inquiry leads naturally to the re-examination of the welfare content of aggregative magnitudes such as G.N.P.[10] In the days of the Keynesian Revolution economists were so preoccupied with the need for employment creation that a bizzare example cited by Keynes of digging a hole in the desert and filling it with greenbacks and city garbages only to be dug up again for 'mining' the greenbacks was in fact taken half seriously by his disciples. Schumpeter's warning at the time that the Keynesian prescription would mean favouring a state of permanent cold war expressed a small minority view in the academic atmosphere dominated then by the oracles of *The General Theory*. But now the academic atmosphere itself is different. Many economists, led by Kenneth Boulding and Joan Robinson, are pointing out the importance of inquiring *how* and *into what type of activities* employment and investment are to be directed; and many others, such as J. Tobin and W. Nordhaus, are engaged in the statistical estimation of a measure of net economic welfare. Admittedly, G.N.P. is a measure of the aggregative economic activities of a country incorporating goods and services currently produced. If 'bads' are produced in the process, they are not subtracted; but 'anti-bads', to the extent currently provided for, are included in the measure of G.N.P. Thus when G.N.P. grows at a very rapid rate, as in the 1960s in Japan, a sizeable amount of 'bads' accompanies the process and the provision of 'anti-bads' becomes necessary, inflating the size of G.N.P. further. It is only natural that attention is now keenly directed towards examining the welfare content of G.N.P. components. The need for this is evinced further by the recognition that 'money votes' in the market by consumers are no longer to be taken as reflecting the true pattern of their preferences. It is true that in that part of the world where even the subsistence requirements are not yet met the exhortation for the rapid growth of G.N.P. has a definite welfare significance. But it is highly questionable if the G.N.P. growth rate can be posited as a welfare target for most of the advanced capitalist countries in the mid–1970s.

For these countries a more basic question is now on the agenda for discussion by economists. That is the problem of what significance we should attach to the saving of labour time in the process of production. E. F. Schumacher made some calculations and came out with a figure of 3·5 per cent as the proportion of 'total social time' spent on actual production in the present-day advanced countries.[11] By 'actual production' he means direct productive activities in agriculture, mining, construction, and industry; and among 'actual producers' he does not include 'people who tell other people what to do, or account for the past, or plan for the future, or distribute what other people have produced'. Then he goes on to observe that

> The process of confining productive time to 3 1/2 percent of total social time has had the inevitable effect of taking all normal human pleasure and satisfaction out of the time spent on this work. Virtually all real production has been turned into an inhuman chore which does not enrich a man but empties him . . . .We may say, therefore, that modern technology has deprived man of the kind of work that he enjoys most, creative, useful work with hands and brains, and given him plenty of work of a fragmented kind, most of which he does not enjoy at all.[12]

The point is well taken; and we may remind ourselves here that the so-called 'productivity drive' in advanced countries today means that capitalists and workers are exhorted to reduce that 3·5 per cent to, let us say, 3·3 or 3·25 per cent. What is the sense of reducing the proportion of 'total social time' spent on actual production if by so doing we make our working hours less pleasant and, on the other hand, are not able to fill up the remaining 90-odd per cent of our time with anything more worthwhile than watching television?

Here is a problem which has been repeatedly raised in one form or another in the course of the development of capitalist societies. In the days of Greek society there used to be a distinction between 'work' – that was performed by free citizens in, for example, making a pot – and 'labour' – that was performed by slaves in, for example, polishing the pot made by free citizens. Nowadays more and more human activity in the process of production is becoming 'labour' rather than 'work'; and it is high time that economists direct their attention to the problem of how satisfying 'labour' actually is and how it can be made more satisfying. In neoclassical economics use is still made of that supply curve of labour where disutility is related to reward, the implication being that the expenditure of labour is a kind of disutility. This peculiar hedonism finds wide application in modern economics, including, for example, its application to the calculation of benefits of a toll highway (or even of a lay-by for sight-seeing purposes!) in terms of the travel time saved. It is not denied that, for some people for certain purposes, the travel time saved could be a saving in pecuniary cost or a source of incremental gain. But the basic question we must ask is *how* we fill the time whether in its use for travel, or for work, or for leisure. One may save ten minutes of travel time by taking a taxi for the distance of a mile as compared with going on foot. One could enjoy, however, walking in the sun, utilising the time for both mental and physical exercise. The welfare intensity of the time, rather than the length of time as such, should be the concern of welfare economics. If we reorientate ourselves in this regard, we may be able to appreciate better what has often been described as an enigmatic aspect of China's road to socialism.[13] In particular, this emphasis on human aspects of daily activities as against technological efficiency as such does constitute a serious challenge to neoclassical paradigms.

Notes and References

Chapter 1 KURT DOPFER

1. Thomas Kuhn, *The Structure of Scientific Revolutions*, 2nd edn (Chicago University Press, 1971); for application to economics see Benjamin Ward, *What's Wrong With Economics?* (New York: Basic Books, 1972) and P. Ady, 'On Economic Advice to Developing Countries', *World Development*, vol. 1, nos 1, 2.

2. For economics as 'the science which studies human behaviour as a relationship between ends and scarce means which have alternative uses' see Lionel Robbins, *An Essay on the Nature and Significance of Economic Science*, 2nd edn (London: Macmillan, 1952).

3. See, for example, Paul A. Samuelson, 'Maximum Principles in Analytical Economics', *American Economic Review*, vol. LXII, no. 3 (June 1972) pp. 249–62.

4. See, for example, J. A. Kregel, *The Reconstruction of Political Economy: an Introduction to Post-Keynesian Economics* (London: Macmillan, 1973) pp. 3–18.

5. William G. Sumner (ed.), *Social Darwinism, Selected Essays* (Englewood Cliffs, N.J.: Prentice-Hall, 1963).

6. For example, J. E. Meade, 'Economic Policy and the Threat of Doom', in *Resources and Population*, ed. B. Benjamin, P. R. Cox and John Peel (London: Academic Press, 1973) p. 120: 'We need to see the system as a whole; and in our present intellectual atmosphere of expert specialization it is precisely in such generalization of interrelationships that we are weakest.'

7. Jan Christian Smuts, *Holism and Evolution* (New York: Greenwood, 1961); J. W. Bews, *Human Ecology* (New York: Russell, 1935); of more recent origin see Michael Polyani, *The Tacit Dimension* (New York: Doubleday-Anchor, 1966). A holistic approach has been developed in other disciplines, for example medicine; see Edward S. Rogers and Harley B. Messinger, 'Human Ecology: Toward a Holistic Method', *Milbank Memorial Fund Quarterly*, vol. XIV, no. 1, pt 1 (Jan 1967); also in I.A.P. Reprints, Health and Education Series, no. 11, East–West Center, Honolulu.

8. Lloyd G. Reynolds, *The Three Worlds of Economics* (Yale University Press, 1971) p. 7.

9. For an introduction see Daniel Suits, *Principles of Economics*, 2nd edn (New York: Harper & Row, 1973) especially ch. entitled 'The Economy as a System'; on General System Theory see Ludwig van Bertalanffy, *General System Theory*,

Foundations, Development, Applications, rev. edn (New York: George Braziller, 1968); A. Rapoport, *Problems and Orientations* (1968); Bertram M. Gross, 'The Coming General Systems Models of Social Systems', *Human Relations* (Nov 1967). For structure and behaviour of systems see Jay W. Forrester, *Principles of Systems*, 2nd edn (Cambridge, Mass.: Wright Allen Press, 1973).

10. We may call this type of system approach a *monistic* system approach; however, there are two types: first, the monistic approach which focuses mainly on automatic versus controlled feedbacks (for example market versus government planning); for a survey see Alexander Eckstein (ed.), *Comparisons of Economic Systems. Theoretical and Methodological Approaches* (California University Press, 1971); the second approach relies mainly on the analysis of positive versus negative feedbacks, excluding the relevant 'modes of operation' as described in the first approach; see, for example, D. H. Meadows *et al.*, *The Limits to Growth* (New York: Universe Books, 1972).

12. I use here the terms 'open' and 'closed' systems different from Kapp and Myrdal (Chapters 6 and 5 respectively). They refer to the system in its relation to other systems defining a 'closed system as one which is not related to other systems; see Bertalanffy, *General System Theory*, pp. 39ff., 139–54. Here a 'closed' system is defined more specifically as one where negative feedbacks control the performance of positive feedbacks, and an 'open' system, where they do not; see, for example, Forrester, *Principles of Systems*, ch. 1.

12. Hans Christoph Binswarger, 'Oekonomie und Oekologie – neue Dimensionen der Wirtschaftstheorie', MS., St Gallen (1973); Ervin Laszlo, 'Reverence for Natural Systems', *Fields Within Fields, Man's Emergent Evolution*, The World Institute, vol. 3, no. 1 (1970); Kenneth E. Boulding, 'Environment and Economics', in *Collected Papers*, vol. III, ed. Boulding (Colorado University Press, 1973).

13. Jan Tinbergen, 'Exhaustion and Technological Development: A Macro-Dynamic Policy Model', MS. (1973).

14. For disagreement see Alexander Gerschenkron, 'History of Economic Doctrines and Economic History', *American Economic Review*, LIX (May 1969) pp. 1–17.

15. Tinbergen, 'Exhaustion and Technological Development'.

16. While a 'new' Schumpeter or Marx is not in sight, the literature on capital accumulation under 'closed' conditions is growing. See, for example, Tjalling C. Koopmans, 'Economic Growth and Exhaustible Resources', in *Economic Structure and Development, Festschrift for Jan Tinbergen*, ed. H. C. Bos *et al.* (Amsterdam: North-Holland, 1973) pp. 239–55; William Nordhaus and James Tobin, 'Is Growth Obsolete?' in *Economic Growth*, ed. Nordhaus and Tobin (New York: National Bureau of Economic Research, 1972) pp. 14–17, 60–70.

17. For example, see John C. H. Fei and Gustav Ranis, 'Economic Development in Historical Perspective', *American Economic Review*, LIX (1969) pp. 386–99; on the feasibility of transferability under (mainly) Asian conditions see Kurt Dopfer, 'The Relationship between Population Growth and Economic Development. A Comparison between 18th and 19th Century Europe and Developing Countries Today', *Journal of Social Science*, no. 12, Tokyo (1974) pp. 43–99.

18. See the pioneering contributions by Harvey Leibenstein, *A Theory of Economic-Demographic Development* (Princeton University Press, 1954) and *Economic Backwardness and Economic Growth* (New York: Wiley, 1957).

19. John C. H. Fei and Gustav Ranis, 'Agrarianisms, Dualisms, and Economic Development', in *The Theory and Design of Economic Development*, ed. Irma Adelman and Erik Thorbecke (Baltimore: Johns Hopkins Press, 1966) pp. 3-41;

having applied a resource framework, the authors conclude that 'we must learn more about tenure and other institutional aspects . . . [and that] what is ultimately needed is a new deterministic transition theory' (p. 40).

20. Oscar Lange, 'The Foundations of Welfare Economics', *Econometrica*, x (1942) pp. 215–28; this article and the one cited in n. 25 are reprinted in *Readings in Welfare Economics*.

21. This proposition is generally accepted in the 'new' welfare economics. However, as Abraham Bergson has shown, value judgements can be formalised and ordered if only the former statement (**A** is preferable to **B**) is considered; see 'A Reformulation of certain aspects of Welfare Economics, *Quarterly Journal of Economics*, 52 (1938) pp. 310–34.

22. See, for example, the proof by Kenneth J. Arrow, *Social Choice and Individual Values*, 2nd edn (Yale University Press, 1963).

23. To my knowledge, the principle of lexical ordering was first re-introduced by John Rawls, *A Theory of Justice* (Oxford University Press, 1971); see p. 42 for a definition; Also, see Laurence H. Tribe, 'Policy Science Analysis or Ideology?', *Philosophy and Public Affairs*, vol. 2, no. 1 (1972) pp. 66–110, reprinted in *Benefit–cost and Policy Analysis* (Chicago: Aldine, 1973).

24. See, for example, Nancy Baster (ed.), *Measuring Development, The Role and Adequacy of Development Indicators* (London: Frank Cass, 1972).

25. On intake needs see, for example, P. V. Sukhatme, 'Human Calorie and Protein Needs and How Far They are satisfied today', in *Resources and Population*, pp. 25–43.

26. The U.N. Conference on the Human Environment in Stockholm (16 May 1972) was the first attempt to establish 'safety limits' for the environment on an international scale.

27. For an interdisciplinary assessment of these categories see Walter Isard *et al.*, *General Theory; Social, Political, Economic and Regional* (Massachusetts Institute of Technology, 1969).

28. See Nordhaus and Tobin, 'Is Growth Obsolete?'; Kenneth Boulding, 'Fun and Games with the Gross National Product. The Role of Misleading Indicators in Social Policy', in *The Environmental Crisis*, ed. Harold W. Helfrich (Yale University Press, 1970) reprinted in *Collected Papers*; Emil Küng, *Wohlstand und Wohlfahrt, Von der Konsumgesellschaft zur Kulturgesellschaft* (Tübingen: Mohr Siebeck, 1972) pp. 3–11, 57–61.

29. Nordhaus and Tobin, 'Is Growth Obsolete?'.

30. Ibid. pp. 4–13.

31. See, for example, Abraham H. Maslow, 'Towards a Humanistic Biology', *Fields Within Fields*, pp. 4–18; and 'A Theory of Metamotivation: The biological rooting of the value-life', *Journal of Humanistic Psychology*, no. 7 (1967) pp. 93–127; also see J. Kamiya, 'Conscious control of brain waves', *Psychology Today*, no. 1 (1968) pp. 56–61, cited by Maslow in the first article in this note.

32. David Ricardo, *On The Principles of Political Economy and Taxation*, in *Collected Works* vol. I, ed. P. Sraffa (Cambridge University Press, 1951) p. 5.

33. Leibenstein, *Theory of Economic-Demographic Development*, ch. II.

34. See, for example, Jan Tinbergen, 'Some Features of the Optimum Regime', in *Optimum Social Welfare and Productivity: A Comparative View*, The Charles C. Moskowitz Lectures (New York University Press, 1972) pp. 21–51.

35. However, even an objective assessment may entail evaluations; for example, the geographer John I. Clark observes: 'Does Africa, for example, suffer from population pressure? Herskovitz, Kamarck, Bohannon, Boserup and Ewing believe that it does. Similar diversity of views exists concerning population pressure

in Britain (Taylor, 1970) and many other parts of the world. Such views will only converge, if we happen to achieve greater unity of values and purpose.' In *Resources and Population*, p. 117.

36. On the possibility of a value verification in economics, see Ward, *What's Wrong with Economics?*, pp. 223–5.

37. An empirical assessment of values has been made, for example, by Seiichiro Saito *et al.*, 'Value System and Social Dynamics, Impact Analysis of Value Changes on Consumption and Industrial Activities', MS., Tokyo (Oct 1973).

38. See, for example, Bruno S. Frey, 'The Politico-Economic System: A Simulation Model', *Kyklos*, vol. XXVII, fasc. 2 (1974) pp. 227–54.

39. For a critique see Silvio Borner, *Auf der Suche nach neuen Grundlagen der Wirtschaftspolitik* (Diessenhofen: Rüegger, 1975).

Chapter 2 JAN TINBERGEN

1. G. Myrdal, *Objectivity in Social Research* (New York: Pantheon Books, 1969).

2. V. M. Dandekar and N. Rath, *Poverty in India* (Bombay, 1971).

3. J. W. Forrester, *World Dynamics* (Cambridge, Mass.: Wright Allen Press, 1971).

4. D. L. Meadows, 'The Predicament of Mankind', *Futurist*, V (1971) p. 137.

5. W. Leontief, 'Air Pollution and the Economic Structure: Empirical Results of Input–Output Computations', Fifth Conference on Input–Output Techniques (Geneva, Jan 1971).

6. J. Tinbergen, 'Two Approaches to the Future: Planning vs. Forecasting' (forthcoming).

7. T. W. Schultz, 'The Distribution of Personal Income; Case Study: The Netherlands', unpublished dissertation, Cambridge, Mass. (1965).

8. See R. H. Tuck, *An Essay on the Economic Theory of Rank* (Oxford: Blackwell, 1954) and B. R. Chiswick, 'Interregional Analysis of Income Distribution' (New York: National Bureau of Economic Research, forthcoming).

9. S.-C. Kolm, *Justice et Equité* (Paris: CEPREMSP, 1971). See also G. Brinkmann, *Berufsanforderungen und Berufsausbildung* (Tübingen-Zürich, 1970).

10. G. C. Hufbauer, 'The Impact of National Characteristics and Technology in the Commodity Composition of Trade in Manufactured Goods', in *The Technology Factor in International Trade*, ed. R. Vernon (New York: National Bureau of Economic Research, 1970).

11. E. J. Mishan, *Welfare Economics: an Assessment* (Amsterdam: North-Holland, 1969).

12. J. Kornai, 'Comment on Professor Tinbergen's Article "Development Strategy and Welfare Economics"', *Coexistence*, 7 (1970) p. 161.

13. J. Van den Doel, *Konvergentie en Evolutie* (Assen: Van Gorcum, 1971).

14. B. Balassa, 'Tariff Reductions and Trade in Manufactures', *American Economic Review*, LVI (1966) p. 466.

15. J. S. Duesenberry, G. Fromm, L. R. Klein and E. Kuh (eds), *The Brookings Quarterly Econometric Model of the United States* (Chicago: Rand McNally, 1965).

16. S. Cohen, *Production, Manpower and Social Planning* (Rotterdam University Press, 1975).

17. C. Duprez and E. S. Kirschen, *Megistos* (Amsterdam: North-Holland, 1970). See also J. L. Mosak, 'Document L39', unpublished document of the United Nations Development Planning Committee.

18. A. F. Burns, *Wesley Mitchell and the National Bureau* (New York: National Bureau of Economic Research, 1949).

19. I. Adelman and C. Taft Morris, 'Performance Criteria for Evaluating Economic Development Potential: An Operational Approach', *Quarterly Journal of Economics*, LXXXII (1968) p. 260.

20. J. Tinbergen, *Meten in de menswetenschappen* (Assen: Van Gorcum, 1971).

21. T. W. Schultz, *The Economic Value of Education* (Columbia University Press, 1963).

22. G. S. Becker, *Human Capital* (New York: National Bureau of Economic Research, 1964).

23. J. Mincer, 'The Distribution of Labor Incomes: A Survey with Special Reference to the Human Capital Approach', *Journal of Economic Literature*, VIII (1970) p. 1 where a long list of references can be found.

24. Schultz, 'The Distribution of Personal Income'.

25. Chiswick, 'Interregional Analysis of Income Distribution'.

26. B. R. Chiswick, 'Earnings Inequality and Economic Development', *Quarterly Journal of Economics*, LXXXV (1971) p. 21.

27. Ibid.; Schultz, *The Economic Value of Education*; and J. Tinbergen, 'Can Income Distribution be Reduced Further?', Festschrift für W. G. Waffenschmidt, Meisenheim an der Glan (1972).

28. L. Soltow, *Towards Income Equality in Norway* (University of Wisconsin Press, 1965).

29. T. Husén, 'Ability, Opportunity and Career', *Education Research*, 10 (1968) p. 170.

30. G. Schmölders, 'Die Ausbildung von technischen Führungskräften für die Wirtschaft', *Zeitschrift für die gesamte Technik*, VDI–Z, 111 (1969) p. 1550.

31. Brinkmann, *Berufsanforderungen und Berufsausbildung*.

32. I. Adelman, 'Short-Run and Long-Run Influences on Income Distribution', mimeo., International Bank for Reconstruction and Development (Washington D.C., 1971).

33. D. B. Fields and W. T. Stanbury, 'Incentives, Disincentives and the Income Tax; Further Empirical Evidence', *Public Finance*, XXV (1970) p. 381.

34. H. B. Chenery, 'Pattern of Industrial Growth', *American Economic Review*, L (1960) p. 624; and H. B. Chenery and H. Hughes, 'The International Division of Labor', European Conference of the Society for International Development (The Hague, 1971).

35. H. Linnemann, *An Econometric Study of International Trade Flows* (Amsterdam: North-Holland, 1966).

36. B. Herman, *A Commodities Classification by Mobility* (Rotterdam: Netherlands Economic Institute, 1971).

37. H. B. Lary, 'Imports of Manufactures from Less Developed Countries', *Studies in International Economic Relations*, 4 (New York: National Bureau of Economic Research, 1968).

38. B. Herman, *On the Problem of the Optimum Use of Factors* (Rotterdam: Netherlands Economic Institute, 1970).

39. B. Herman and J. Tinbeigen, 'Planning of International Development' (Budapest, forthcoming).

40. G. M. Meier, *Leading Issues in Economic Development*, 2nd edn (Oxford University Press, 1970) p. 593.

41. H. S. Houthakker and J. Tobin, 'Estimates of the Free Demand for Rationed Foodstuffs', *Economic Journal*, 62 (1952) p. 103.

Chapter 3 HARVEY LEIBENSTEIN

1. This section summarises some ideas elaborated in the following; H. Leibenstein, 'Allocative Efficiency vs. X-Efficiency', *American Economic Review*, LVI (June 1966); 'Organizational or Frictional Equilibria, X-Efficiency and the Rate of Innovation', *Quarterly Journal of Economics*, 83 (Nov 1969); 'Competition and X-Efficiency: Reply', *Journal of Political Economy*, vol. 81, no. 3 (May–June 1973).

2. See W. S. Comanor and Harvey Leibenstein, 'Allocative Efficiency, X-Efficiency and the Measurement of Welfare Losses', *Economica* (Aug 1969) for a more elaborate treatment of these ideas.

3. See Leibenstein, 'X-Efficiency and the Rate of Innovation'.

4. An excellent summary of the contributions of the Carnegie School can be found in K. J. Cohen and R. M. Cyert, *Theory of the Firm: Resource Allocation in a Market Economy* (Englewood Cliffs, N.J.: Prentice-Hall, 1965) chs 16–17.

Chapter 6 K. WILLIAM KAPP

1. Michael J. Perelman, 'Farming with Petroleum', *Environment*, vol. 14 (8) pp. 8–13 (Oct 1972).

2. It has been estimated that the Chinese wet-rice farmer gets for each unit of energy expended more than 50 units of energy in returns; 'for each unit of fossil unit of energy we expend in the U.S. we get about one fifth in return. On the basis of these two ratios, Chinese wet rice agriculture is far more "efficient" than our own system'; ibid. p. 12.

3. Luc Bigler, 'Zur Stagnation der "Grünen Revolution" – Sozioökonomische Hemmungsfaktoren in der Diffusion neuer Technologien in Entwicklungsländern dargestellt am Beispiel der Verwendung von High Yielding Varieties in der indischen Landwirtschaft', Basler dissertation, unpublished (1974).

4. Additional dollar returns from additional applications of pesticides are estimated to vary from \$2·82 to \$4–5 per dollar spent on pesticides; David Pimentel, 'Realities of a Pesticide Ban', *Environment*, vol. 15 (2) (Mar 1973) p. 25.

5. Perelman, 'Farming with Petroleum', p. 13.

6. Such as the use of parasites, pathogens, predators, chemical and physical attractants, sterile males and genetic manipulations. On this subject and some notable failures of pesticides to eradicate pests, including those causing malaria, see the work of the Commonwealth Institute of Biological Control with headquarters in Trinidad and various stations throughout the British Commonwealth plus a European station in Delémont (Switzerland) as well as the following publications: Hubert Pschorn-Walcher, 'Probleme der biologischen Bekämpfung eingeschleppter Pflanzenschädlinge', *Biologie in unserer Zeit*, 2 (June 1972) pp. 67–75; Richard Garcia, 'The Control of Malaria', *Environment*, 14, no. 5 (June 1972) pp. 2–9; Göran Lofroth, 'Who cares about DDT', *Ecologist*, 1, no. 17 (Nov 1971) pp. 8–9.

7. On the whole subject see Pimental, 'Realities of a Pesticide Ban', pp. 28–9.

8. R. L. Ackoff, 'Systems, Organizations and Interdisciplinary Research', *General Systems Yearbook*, vol. 5 (1960) p. 1.

9. Ibid. p. 1.

10. C. D. Darlington, *The Conflict of Society and Science* (London: Watts, 1948) quoted from John Dewey, *Reconstruction of Philosophy* (New York: Mentor, 1948) p. 14.

11. Ibid. p. 14.

12. As Darlington pointed out with references to new developments in the natural sciences, 'it is no accident that bacteria were first understood by a canal engineer, that oxygen was isolated by a Unitarian minister, that the theory of infection was established by a chemist, the theory of heredity by a monastic school teacher, and the theory of evolution by a man who was unfitted to be a university instructor in either botany or zoology', and, Darlington added, the great innovators 'are the first to fear and doubt their discoveries'; ibid. pp. 14–15.

13. René Dubos, 'Review of Barry Commoner, The Closing Circle', *Environment*, vol. 14, no. 1 (Jan–Feb 1972) p. 48.

14. In lieu of a detailed bibliography we must confine ourselves to listing a few key names: A. N. Whitehead, John Dewey, Joseph Needham, Thorstein Veblen, L. A. Kroeber, Gunnar Myrdal, L. von Bertalanffy. For further details cf. K. William Kapp, *Towards a Science of Man in Society* (The Hague: Nizlioff, 1961).

15. Cf. Alan Coddington, 'The Economics of Ecology', *New Society* (Apr 1970) pp. 595–7.

16. So far very little attention has been paid to these cumulative causal processes; the great exceptions are of course the institutionalists such as Veblen and Myrdal. For an analysis of their key concepts of circular interdependencies and cumulative causation within the context of economics as a subsystem of the socio-cultural institutional composite system, see K. William Kapp, 'In Defense of Institutionalism', *Swedish Journal of Economics*, vol. LXX, no. 1 (1968) pp. 1–18.

17. David W. Fischer, 'On the Problems of Measuring Environmental Benefits and Costs', *Social Science Information*, 13, 2 (1973) p. 104.

18. Ibid. p. 8. Cf. also H. H. Liebhafsky, *The Nature of Price Theory* (Homewood, Ill.: Dorsey, 1968) p. 266.

19. Cf. K. William Kapp, 'Social Costs, Neo-Classical Economists, Environmental Planning: A Reply', *Environmental Policies and Development Planning in Contemporary China and Other Essays* (Paris: Mouton, 1974) pp. 99ff.

20. For a distinction of social (including environmental) indicators and norms, see ibid. pp. 127–38.

21. This brings our notion of normative economics close to that of political economics: the theory of controlled economic systems as developed by Adolf Loewe, *Economic Knowledge* (New York: Harper & Row, 1965); Cf. also R. L. Heilbronner, 'On the Possibility of Political Economics', *Journal of Economic Issues*, IV, 4 (1970) and François Hetman, *Society and the Assessment of Technology* (Paris: O.E.C.D., 1973) pp. 379–90, esp. p. 389.

22. For a formal demonstration of this incompatibility, see David Pearce, 'An Incompatibility in Planning for a Steady State and Planning for Maximum Economic Welfare', *Environment and Planning*, vol. 5 (1973) pp. 267–71; and, by the same author, 'Economics and Ecology', *Survey Papers in Economics*, no. 10 (1974).

23. 'L'écologie est intégrée sans douleur par la théorie néo-classique et la Nature devient un secteur économique susceptible d'être comptabilisé dans les schémas rassurants de l'équilibre'. Jan Dessau, 'Modèles dualistes de l'Environnement et Choix de Techniques'; paper presented at Symposium International, Analyse socio-économique de l'Environnement, Problèmes de Méthodes, Grenoble Conférence, mimeo. (1972) p. 8.

24. 'Loosely speaking, no argument on economic matters will get a reasonable

wide hearing until it is set out as a "business proposition" in terms drawn from the conduct of business administration, business finance, national trade, salesmanship and publicity', Thorstein Veblen, 'Economic Theory in the Calculable Future', *American Economic Review*, vol. xv, no. 1, supplement (Mar 1925) p. 53.

25. J. J. Spengler, 'Economics: Its History, Themes, Approaches', *Journal of Economic Issues*, 2 (Mar 1968) p. 21.

Chapter 7 SHIGETO TSURU

1. Paul A. Samuelson, *Economics*, 9th edn (New York: McGraw-Hill, 1973) p. 533.
2. Ibid. p. 499.
3. O. Lange and F. M. Taylor, *On the Economic Theory of Socialism* (Minnesota University Press, 1938) pp. 103–4.
4. Allen V. Kneese, 'The Faustian Bargain', *Resources*, no. 44, Resources for the Future (Sep 1973) p. 1.
5. Adam Smith, *The Nature and Causes of the Wealth of Nations* (New York: The Modern Library, 1937) p. 423.
6. Karl Marx, *Grundrisse der Kritik der politischen Oekonomie* (Berlin: Dietz Verlag, 1953) pp. 592ff.
7. This is typically a cost-push situation which tends to be the more inflationary the more rapid the productivity rise is in the leading industries within the 'planning system'. In such a situation, Paul Samuelson admits, macroeconomic fiscal and monetary policies are insufficient and some kind of 'incomes policy' is needed. But he himself confesses quite candidly that 'in the current state of knowledge about the modern mixed economy, no jury of competent economists can reach broad agreement on how to recommend a feasible and optimal incomes policy' (Samuelson, *Economics*, p. 825). It may be stated, however, that unless we grasp the implications of the changing mode of production as conditioned by the development of productive forces we will not be able to start tackling the present-day problem of creeping inflation in any effective way.
8. J. K. Galbraith, *Economics and the Public Purpose* (Boston: Houghton Mifflin, 1973) p. 91.
9. F. H. Knight, 'Some Fallacies in the Interpretation of Social Cost', *Quarterly Journal* (1924), reprinted in K. J. Arrow and T. Scitovsky, *Readings in Welfare Economics* (Homewood, Ill.: Irwin, 1969) pp. 226–7.
10. Since I discussed this topic already in my earlier paper – 'In Place of G.N.P.', *Social Science Information* (Aug 1971) – I shall be brief here.
11. E. F. Schumacher, *Small Is Beautiful* (London: Blond & Briggs, 1973) pp. 130–40.
12. Ibid. p. 140.
13. A competent, sympathetic account of Chinese socialism is given in E. L. Wheelwright and Bruce McFarlane, *The Chinese Road to Socialism – Economics of the Cultural Revolution* (New York: Monthly Review Press, 1970).